THE

THE NEW LINE TO LONDON

OF THE

GREAT CENTRAL RAILWAY

CENTENARY EDITION

1899 - 1999

A REPORT ON THE CONSTRUCTION AND FORMAL OPENING

OF THE EXTENSION FROM ANNESLEY, NOTTINGHAM,

TO LONDON MARYLEBONE

FRIDAY, MARCH 10th., 1899

Edited by

MICHAEL J. SOAR

THE NEW LINE TO LONDON

OF THE

GREAT CENTRAL RAILWAY

CENTENARY EDITION

1899 - 1999

ISBN 0 9536526 0 2

Published in England by

Rook Books,
16 The Green,
Chilwell,
Nottinghamshire,
NG9 5BE.
Tel: 01159 - 259380

Printed in England by

Ram Print Limited,
Kingsway Park Close,
Kingsway Industrial Park,
Derby,
DE22 3FT.
Tel: 01332 - 345950

FOREWORD

by

Dr. David A. Clarke, Hon. D. Tech.

President of Great Central Railway PLC

Finding something of historical importance is a wonderful achievement in itself - to discover archive material if the subject is interesting to the finder and, better still, is equally interesting to others is even more valuable. Our heritage, our inventions, our achievements, struggles, heartaches, even our sadnesses and losses are all part of our wonderful history.

Those interested in railways can all share in the pride we must genuinely feel about the pioneering work carried out in this country, the true birthplace of steam railways, which, like other forms of transport on land, sea and air, have progressed at a tremendous rate over the years. For so long steam was King; even so it had to give way to diesel and electricity after close on one and a half centuries of efficient operation, but what a wonderful memory it left behind not only in preservation but, also, in pictorial and written form as well.

How lucky we are that so very many like-minded and caring people had the foresight to ensure that the history of our beloved railways was so comprehensively cared for. To them I give my heartfelt thanks and congratulations, none more so than to Mike Soar who has painstakingly sifted through those old documents to put together such enjoyable reading.

You will not have to be a railway enthusiast to enjoy this wonderful book but, if you are, then it will be more enjoyable still.

Ulverscroft Grange
14th. July 1999

ACKNOWLEDGEMENTS

The contents of this book are reproduced courtesy of the Nottingham Evening Post and I am indebted to the Editor and his staff for their support.

I am grateful for the help and encouragement of the directors, management and members of Main Line Steam Trust Limited, Great Central Railway plc, and Great Central Railway (Nottingham) Limited.

My thanks for the guidance received from the editorial staff at Steam Railway magazine.

The G.C.R. Coat of Arms is reproduced by permission of Great Central Railway plc.

Michael J. Soar
June 1999

THE NEW LINE TO LONDON

CONTENTS

ILLUSTRATIONS

PREFACE

Late in 1996 a friend gave me a carrier bag saying, "I found this when I was clearing out my uncle's house - thought it might interest you - something to do with trains." The bag contained part of the Nottingham Daily Guardian, dated Friday, 10th. March 1899, consisting of four broadsheet pages of close type. Needless to say it was in a very poor state but, with the aid of a domestic iron and adhesive tape, I managed to piece it together. The result looked somewhat moth eaten and the paper continued to flake.

The story of the day was about the construction and formal opening of the Great Central Railway extension from Annesley, Nottingham, to Marylebone - The New Line to London. As I read the article I realised it was something of historical significance that was worth preserving - I was hooked! I photocopied the illustrations, clamped the pages between sheets of clear perspex, and set about transcribing the text onto my computer.

By early 1997 I had completed the task, over 35,000 words, and thought that I would write a book for the centenary year. However one thing niggled me - what had been written in the spaces? It was like finishing a jigsaw puzzle only to find several pieces missing - should I call it complete or search for those missing pieces?

Curiosity prevailed and I started my research in the central library in Nottingham. Fortunately there was a micro-film copy of the newspaper which, although poorer and darker than my copy, contained much of the lost text. This was time consuming work, using a magnifying glass, which could only be undertaken for short periods to avoid eye strain. Next I turned to the works of George Dow and, thence, to other books and sources of information. Amongst the more difficult details to locate were the names of people, such as civic dignitaries, who had taken part in the parliamentary hearings and those who had been invited to the formal luncheon and opening ceremony at Marylebone station.

A year later, in 1998, the text was complete but I faced another dilemma. I was immersed so totally in what had been written a hundred years ago that to consider writing a new book would detract from the nature of what I had set out to preserve. Only by keeping to the language of the day, with its style, punctuation and spelling, could the book evoke the atmosphere and spirit of the late Victorian era so I decided to produce it in a format that was as close as possible to that presented to the public in March 1899.

I am grateful for the encouragement I have received from many people over the past two years and now, in June 1999, I am able to write this preface in the hope that all who read the story will get as much pleasure from it as I have had in preserving it for future generations.

Mike Soar

The Headlines of the Day

NOTTINGHAM DAILY GUARDIAN, FRIDAY, MARCH 10th, 1899.

THE NEW LINE TO LONDON

OPENING CEREMONY

HISTORY OF THE UNDERTAKING

PARLIAMENTARY STRUGGLES

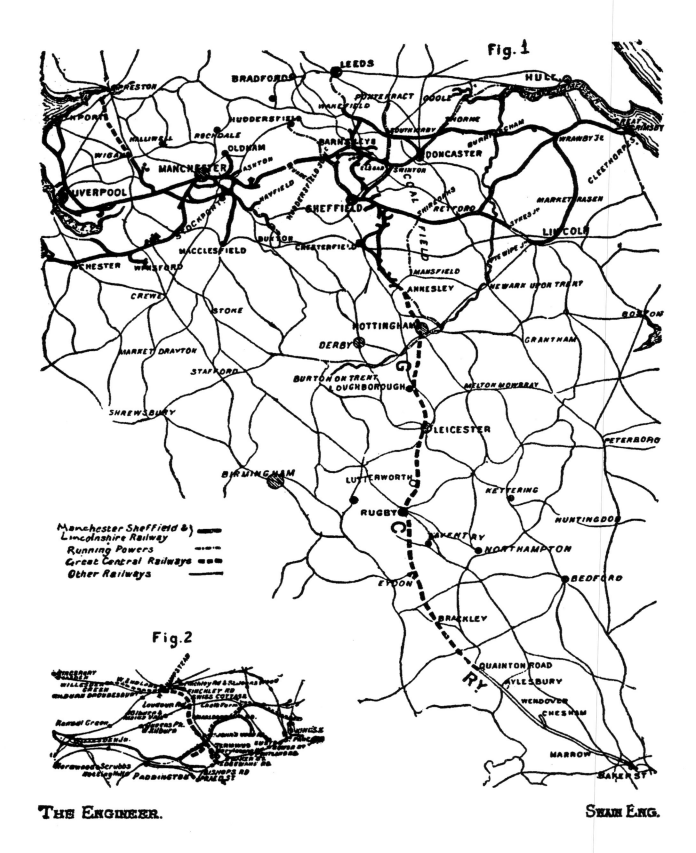

MAP OF THE ROUTE

SOME NOTABLE FACTS

In the history of British railway undertakings yesterday's ceremony in connection with the formal opening of the new line to London of the Great Central Railway Company is destined to remain memorable. By reason of the far-reaching considerations involved, the completion of the new trunk route to the Metropolis ranks as one of the most important projects of the kind which has been effected in the latter part of the present century.

In a significant speech Sir Edward Watkin once declared that he and those associated with him would never rest content until the old Sheffield company was landed in London. The doyen of railway directorates has happily lived to witness the outcome for which he laboured incessantly as affording the only sound means of rehabilitating the finances of the M., S., and L., now known by its more comprehensive title as the Great Central Company.

The influence of the new railway upon Nottingham and the district can scarcely be over-estimated. Whilst affording a new passenger route to London, the scheme is destined to prove of even greater importance in relation to mineral traffic. The extension of the old system was vital in the interests of the general body of the shareholders, whilst benefiting large and important districts by the establishment of a new trunk route. The Great Central has been for years in the unfortunate position of having to hand over to other companies the bulk of their through traffic with merchandise and mineral before they had carried it through any distance. The aggregate receipts of the Central Company from traffic interchanged with other companies has been about one-third only, the remaining two-thirds being taken by other companies, and bearing in mind the fact that the gross receipts from through traffic for 1891 were £3,275,089, it will be realised how large a sum has had to be handed over to other undertakings.

It has cost the company six and a half millions to get to London, but judging from the tone of speeches which have been heard upon more than one occasion at the half yearly meetings at Manchester, few of the representative shareholders have any want of faith as to the ultimate result of the outlay.

The first link in the important chain of extension was formed by the line between Beighton and Annesley. By this means the Great Central obtained for the first time independent access to the rich coalfield of the Leen Valley, while being enabled by running powers over the Great Northern line into Nottingham to reach the county town both for goods and passenger purposes.

From Annesley to Quainton road, the further important development, covering the intervening space of 92 miles 18 chains, has now taken place, affording the possibility, in conjunction, for the present, with the Metropolitan line, but ultimately with the Great Western, of reaching the Metropolis. It has a line opening up large and growing districts. It has not, however, been without a series of most stubborn Parliamentary battles that the necessary powers have been obtained to enable the company to accomplish the great aim which the directors have had for so many years in view.

The first Bill under which the company sought to obtain authority to widen their scope of influence came before Parliament about ten years ago. An attempt had been made to effect an arrangement with the Midland, but the two companies were unable to arrive at an understanding. When the Bill came before the Committee of the House of Commons the Midland suggested that certain running powers should be granted to the Great Central, and coming to the conclusion that this would afford the latter company all they desired to obtain, the Committee rejected the Bill.

The directors of the Great Central, however, were of the opinion that such an arrangement as proposed would be one of little practical use to them and under further pressure from a large body of traders for through rates, they decided, as a preliminary to the larger scheme which was contemplating to promote a system of railways from Beighton Junction, going into Staveley and Chesterfield through the coal districts, down to Annesley where a junction would be effected with the Leen Valley branch of the Great Northern. This application was heard by a Special Committee of the House of Commons, presided over by Sir John Kennaway, Bart. in May, 1889, and it had the support of a number of influential public bodies and property owners in Notts., Derbyshire, and other localities affected by the scheme. By the proposal powers were sought to construct the line through Staveley and Chesterfield, thence to run in a southerly direction to the Leen Valley, opening up a communication with various large collieries and ironworks en route, including those at Holbrook, Norwood, Renishaw, Markham, Holmeswood, Pilsley, Tibshelf, Staveley and New Hucknall.

The principal opponents of the proposal were the Midland Company, who contended that all the proposed railways were designed to compete with existing Midland lines, and together to form a system of railways in parallel and in great part closely adjoining the Midland Railway from Beighton to Chesterfield and also to several branch lines constructed by the Midland Company, and acquired for the development in connection with their railway of the coal and iron industries of the district. They were willing, in accordance with an offer made some time previously to accord the petitioners reasonable running powers over the Midland line to Chesterfield, and they submitted that under such circumstances the construction of unnecessary duplicate lines ought not to receive sanction of Parliament. Certainly the proposed railways were not, they contended, required to meet any public necessity, but were meant solely to enable the Great Central or the Great Northern to compete with the Midland for the traffic of the district. The objectors to the Bill further said that they had incurred a very large expenditure in providing railway accommodation for the development of the coal and iron trades of the district traversed by the proposed railways, and that it would be therefore unfair to them and not to the public interest that, by the sanction of Parliament being given to a new competing route, they should be deprived of a fair return on the outlay they had made.

The Great Northern Company had also filed a petition against the Bill, in which they urged that the new railways were unnecessary, and the effect of their construction would be to divert traffic from the Great Northern line.

In opening the case for the petitioners councel pointed out that the Great Central had a large interest in the collieries of the Derbyshire districts, and at the present time the only communication which they had with them was by means of a junction with the Midland line at Beighton. The company possessed no powers south of Beighton, and for the whole district below that they were dependent on the Midland Company, although they did run certain trains themselves. The greater part of the scheme had been submitted to the House the previous year, but the portion running south of Annesley, which was very important, was not then included. It would be entirely useless to the Great Central to have merely running powers over the Midland. They desired a separate line, and now came there with their proposal backed by the opinion of most of the people in the district. The scheme was supported by the Corporations of Nottingham, Sheffield, and Chesterfield, and the London and North Western Railway Company also endorsed the proposal.

So far as the Great Northern Company were concerned, the Great Central proposed to give them, like the London and North Western, running powers affording them direct communication with Sheffield, with liberty to fix their own rates, on the condition that the Great Northern afforded them running powers over the Leen Valley to Nottingham. There was not a single landowner in the district who was opposing the scheme.

It was said by the Midland Company that they were willing to afford the Great Central all the accommodation necessary, but the traffic of the district was immense and could not be adequately worked from the point of view of petitioners unless they were allowed to construct a line of their own, and there was plenty of room for them as well as the Midland.

Evidence in support of the Bill was given from Sheffield, by the Lord Mayor (Ald. W. J. Clegg), the Master Cutler (Mr. S. E. Howell), the secretary of the Chamber of Commerce, and other witnesses from Chesterfield, Staveley, Renishaw, Eckington, and Brimington, as well as by representatives of various colliery owners and companies in Derbyshire, Leicestershire and Nottinghamshire. In connection with the collieries at Tibshelf, Mr. Charles Hilton Seely, M.P., strongly supported the scheme, as offering larger and increased facilities, although he did not complain of the manner in which the Midland Company had conducted their traffic. Mr. Bainbridge, as managing director of the Blackwell and New Hucknall Collieries, Mr. Hugh Brown, of Nottingham, as owner of property at South Normanton, Mr. Walter Salmond, J.P., general manager of the Pinxton Collieries, also supported the Bill, and were followed by Ald. Renals (then Mayor of Nottingham), who expressed the sentiment of the Town Council that the new line would be of great advantage to the town, regarding the projected line as supplying an alternative route to Sheffield, and tending to open out entirely new districts. On general principal he and the Council favoured the introduction of any new railway, as increased facilities must benefit the community. Sir Samuel Johnson, Town Clerk, agreed with the opinions expressed by the Mayor, while Sir John Turney said that in his judgment the proposed line would be of great utility to the district through which it passed, and also to Nottingham. Ald. Gripper, J.P., as ex-Mayor of the borough, said it would be a considerable advantage to Nottingham to have an alternative railway route, for trade purposes particularly. Mr. Robert Mellors also thought Nottingham would be considerably benefited thereby.

During the cross-examination of Mr. Pollitt, the general manager of the Great Central, a remark fell from Sir John Kennaway which, in the light of present developments, is rather interesting. The Chairman said he saw that the Great Northern Company credited the Great Central with much greater intentions as to extension than going to Nottingham, namely, that they were going to London, an observation which was received with laughter.

On behalf of the Midland Company, the late Mr. John Noble, then general manager, stated that their line down to Annesley was not so overcrowded that they could not accommodate the Great Central. As regarded the northern portion of the line, he contended that the running powers that the Midland offered absolutely covered the whole ground, whilst to the southern part there was really no case for it. Councel for the Midland put forward the claims of the company for proper protection. He did not venture to suggest that the Midland had a monopoly, but he did say that when a company had spent its capital and laid itself out to accommodate a district, and had done that well, they ought not to be unduly interfered with. He characterised the claim of the Great Central as simply the same as was rejected the previous year, and that nothing had been put before the Committee to justify them in coming to a different conclusion. He submitted that the whole public case of the Bill would be met by running powers over the northern portion of the Midland system, with the right to use their colliery branches.

In addressing the Committee on behalf of the Great Northern Company, councel drew attention to the fact that whilst the Great Central was slowly creeping southwards the Metropolitan was gradually creeping north, and by a line they were promoting that session the distance separating them would only be 60 miles. Under an agreement of 1860 between the Great Northern and Great Central, it was agreed that the latter should not project a line further south than Nottingham, nor the former go further west than Retford in the direction of Sheffield and Manchester. It was true that that agreement had been abrogated by mutual consent, but it existed for all practical purposes, and the Great Northern merely asked that it should continue to be observed for the next twenty years, during which the original agreement would have obtained. If the Great Central did not want to get further south and to London, why need they object to the suggestion? But the fact was that that was their object, and under those circumstances he asked the Committee to protect the Great Northern by renewing the agreement of 1860.

Counsel for the petitioners characterised the arguments on behalf of the Great Northern as monstrously unfair, and the offer of the Midland with regard to running powers as practically useless, as colliery proprietors and the traders would still be in the hands of the Midland.

Eventually the Committee considered the preamble of the Bill proved, with the exception of a portion relating to a small branch to Holmeswood Colliery.

No time was lost in proceeding with the work, and the ceremony of cutting the first sod, which took place at Beighton Junction some months later, was attended by a large and influential company, who were subsequently entertained by the directors at a banquet held at the Victoria Hotel, Sheffield, under the presidency of Sir Edward Watkin, among the speakers being the Master Cutler of Sheffield and Sir John Turney.

THE LARGER SCHEME

AN ABORTIVE APPLICATION

Severe as was the struggle over the 1889 Bill, for more important issues were involved by the application made by the company two years later for Parliamentary powers to make the extension from Annesley onwards to London, the scheme which has now been carried into effect. The application was heard by a Committee of the House of Commons, presided over by Mr. Woodall, and the contentious nature of the proceedings is indicated by the fact that the enquiry extended over a period of two months, though that included the Whitsuntide recess, and that over 20 interests were represented by councel before Committee.

The object of the measure, as set out in the detail, was to authorise the company to construct extension railways, commencing from Kirkby-in-Ashfield, passing through Nottingham, by Loughborough, Leicester, Lutterworth, and Brackley, to Aylesbury and Buckingham railway at Quainton; certain deviation of authorised lines at the commencement of the railway; and extension into the suburbs of London from the Metropolitan Railway (St. John's Wood line) at Willesden Green Station, to a terminal station adjoining Boscobel Gardens at Marylebone; the railway to constitute a separate undertaking of the company; and to authorise the payment of interest out of capital during the construction of the works.

In the course of an exhaustive opening for the petitioners, councel traced the history and development of the Great Central system. The company was, he explained, originally constructed for Manchester and Sheffield, but they had carried out a large number of extensions themselves, and by means of their allies. One thing they did was to establish docks at Grimsby. The first dock there was a very humble undertaking, as Grimsby was then a mere fishing village, but at the time of this, the latest petition to Parliament, the docks and kindred works had become so extensive, at a cost of something like 2½ millions, that an enormous trade had been developed. Altogether the railway system of the promoters then covered about 500 miles, and something like 28½ millions had been spent upon it.

At Grimsby the previous year they imported 489,000 tons of general traffic, exclusive of fish; there was an extra 780,000 tons of coal and 98,000 tons of Grimsby produce. The company also had a line of sea-going steamers, and had altogether done an enormous amount of work in improving the trade and industries of the country, while Grimsby had been so developed that it had become the largest fishing port in the world.

In 1864 the South Yorkshire line, which had been laid for the development of the coal industry, was purchased by the petitioners, and had become an integral part of the system. One of the chief arguments in the case of the promoters was that they had been badly placed in the matter of long distance routes, which were the paying routes. A large portion of the South Yorkshire coal went to London, which the promoters were obliged to hand over to the Great Northern and the Midland, with the result that though they collected the traffic they did not get anything like the amount of profit out of it that was got by the other lines. As time had gone on that traffic had enormously developed, and they had absolutely enormous sidings for the purpose of dealing with the coal trade before it left their system. But they had to do the work without getting any appreciable advantage, the other great companies getting the largest proportion of the profits which arose from the traffic. That was a statement which applied, more or less, to the whole of the Great Central system.

Taking 1890 as an example, out of the total receipts arising from the traffic originating on the Great Central their share was not greater than one-third, the percentage being 32.87 on £3,129,000. The docks at Grimsby although they cost two and a half millions of money, did not pay owing to the short length of line belonging to the Great Central over which the produce was carried, and yet the company were being pressed for the provision of still further facilities for dealing with the fishing traffic. There was already in existence at Grimsby very excellent accommodation, but it was altogether insufficient. The Great Central had asked the other companies if they would make some allowance to them in view of the long length of line over which that traffic ran, so far as the other companies were concerned, after it left the Great Central system, but they had always refused.

Another point was that there was not a single place over their whole system where they were not competed with, so that they had no opportunity of making up for the loss of traffic caused by the competitive traffic, by levying higher rates on non-competitive traffic. That being the case the Great Central, about three years before, began to do what they might advisedly have done before. The company had been pressed by traders for through rates. They tried their best to get a satisfactory arrangement with the Midland Company, but could get nothing out of them. So in 1889 they promoted a Bill to meet the requirements of the traders, and it was then, for the first time in their experience that the Midland made an offer. They suggested that the Great Central should be given running powers, and the committee of the House of Commons being of the opinion that they could get all they wanted by those means rejected the Bill with permission to run over the Midland. The Great Central, feeling that that would be of no possible use to them, refused to accept those terms.

After that the traders pressed more than ever, and ultimately the company decided to promote a system of railways going into Chesterfield from the coal districts, down to Annesley, with the result which has been already described. Having got that extension to Annesley they gave the London and North-Western Company running powers over that line as the price for their not further promoting a line which they had proposed to carry into Sheffield. The London and North-Western, however, never exercised those powers, being quite content with the way in which the Great Central dealt with the traffic, which they sent over their line.

The Great Northern which had hitherto opposed all their extensions, then said to them that they would oppose no longer if they did not go further south. But for years they had been pressed by the coalowners and other people to carry on their lines to the south, and consequently they had prepared that scheme. The proposed line would not make much appreciable difference as to distances, in fact the distances were sometimes against them, but they could cover the ground in the same time, and the advantage to be derived would be the increased convenience to the public. It would be a very workable express line, inasmuch as with one single exception it would have no gradient more severe than 1 in 100. The cost, including borrowing powers, would be in round figures 6¼ millions sterling.

With regard to the question of whether the venture would pay the company had no fear. Taking the whole of their line the receipts per mile the previous year was £6,760, or £130 per week, and if they obtained the same average for the 97 miles of the new line - and there was no reason why they should not - that would give a gross income of £656,000. Taking the working expenses at 50 per cent., that would leave them about £328,000, and that on the capital authorised by the Bill would enable the payment of a dividend of 5.13 per cent. That would obviously give them such an income as would justify the construction of the line. The company had 28 millions of capital, most of it in preference shares, and they asked the committee to allow them, during the construction of the line, to pay a reasonable rate of interest.

That the Great Central were keeping abreast of the times was demonstrated by the fact that in the last 20 years they had spent eleven and a half millions in developing traffic, and in the last 15 years there had been a sufficiently large increase from Nottingham alone to pay for the construction of the proposed extension.

Without complaining of the Great Northern the promoters had a certain amount to put up with from that company, and they desired to relieve themselves of the inconveniences and difficulties they were subject to. The Midland Railway petition against the scheme was based entirely upon a protest against the increased competition of the Great Central, but it must be remembered, councel said, that the Midland Company had made itself by its extensions, extensions made in direct competition with existing railways.

The petition of the Great Northern was framed, it was argued, for the purpose of prejudicing the Great Central with the Committee, and it contained allegations which were perfectly astonishing. The suggestion that the amount of traffic would not be sufficient to justify the outlay of the proposed capital was characterised as being ungenerous. The system of the Great Northern was at that time congested with traffic, and it was contended they ought not to object to anything in the shape of friendly rivalry on the part of a friendly railway company. Both would have plenty of traffic to deal with after the extension of the Great Central system, and the Great Northern would not suffer for the reason that new traffic would be developed along the new route.

The Great Northern also alleged that the financial history of the Great Central in the past did not justify them being entrusted with so great an expenditure, but that, councel observed, was rather a cool way of speaking of a company that had expended 28 millions of capital and with which the Great Northern had themselves entered into agreements. There were few companies who would have had the courage to make the docks at Grimsby and the connections between east and west, and having spent so much were entitled to ask that they should not be trampled upon by their opponents, but should reap their legitimate reward.

The opening up of the South Yorkshire and Notts. coalfields was the first aspect of the scheme dealt with in evidence, and in this connection Mr. J. R. Hewitt, F.G.S., stated that the coal measures which the Committee had heard of as being north of Nottingham would be found to extend also ten miles south. The new line would pass through an undeveloped coalfield of 120 square miles. Coal had been found at over 600 yards depth, and the thickness of the seam was four or five feet. He did not know at what depth the same seam was worked in the Leen Valley. He did not think there were more collieries in the Leen Valley than there were 15 years before, and those existing had reached their maximum development. He believed the coal dipped rather south of Nottingham, and when borings had gone on it had been found where it was expected, and where it would naturally be found when the seams north and south of Nottingham were continuous.

Mr. Charles Tylden Wright informed the Committee that the continuous coalfield under the proposed line had been proved, and agreed with Mr. Hewitt as to the nature and extent of the undeveloped coal in south Notts. They looked to that district to take the place of other coal measures which would be exhausted within twenty years.

Other evidence was as to the effect that the new line would produce on the output of coal would be that all through Derbyshire and Notts., and a good deal of Yorkshire, during the next 14 or 15 years the quantity of coal obtained would be doubled.

Sir Samuel Johnson, in the course of a lengthy examination, stated that the Town Council of Nottingham were entirely in favour of the scheme, together with the inhabitants generally. The new line would give Nottingham what it had long desired, a central station. For many years they had been endeavouring to get the other companies to give them a central station, the advantages of which they considered very necessary and very desirable. In 1875 they asked the Great Northern Company for a central station, and offered them a very extensive site for the purpose, as a matter of fact, the site of the cattle market, but without result. Afterwards they approached the Midland and the L. and N. W. Companies, and proposed to give them the site of the old gaol, but again without result. The scheme promoted for the extension of the Great Central would give the town all it desired, and the manufacturers and traders of Nottingham were strongly of opinion that the extension would be to their advantage. What they wanted was a direct route to London.

At that time they were practically in the hands of the Midland Company, and even then they were not on a main trunk line, whereas by the proposed scheme they would be placed on a main through line. A town like Nottingham ought not to be dependent on one railway, and they would like to have a station in a central position which could be used by all the three competing lines, although such a proposition had come to nothing. The line would go through a thickly populated part of the town, and it would chop up certain streets, but none of them were important ones, and if the company did not take them down the Corporation would have to sweep them away before long. He did not think any railway could be brought into the centre of Nottingham and disturb things less than the proposed line would.

Sir John Turney and Ald. S. H. Sands, then Mayor of the town, expressed themselves strongly in favour of the scheme, and concurred with the Town Clerk's evidence in its entirety, the latter adding that the proposed line would lead to a considerable increase of the trade and the traffic of Nottingham, particularly the coal industry. It would give greater facilities in reaching the town from Basford on the north, and Loughborough on the south, and would develop several places ultimately into residential suburbs. It would also give them direct communication with Huddersfield and the West Yorkshire district without any change of train. The hosiery and yarn, which formed so large a part of the material used in the trade of Nottingham, came from that district, and it was unquestionable that better communication was needed between Nottingham and the West Yorkshire district.

Mr. Thomas Birkin gave evidence as to the necessities of Ruddington in particular, and explained that a large proportion of its population was engaged in the hosiery trade, one-sixth only being agricultural. In the census of 1881 the population was between 2,500 and 2,600, but it had since somewhat declined. He attributed the decline to hand made hosiery being superseded by power machines. If the Bill passed, Ruddington would be put on direct and easy communication with Nottingham and a large number of factories would in his opinion be built there. The people engaged in agriculture would also have an advantage in transmitting their produce. A line with local stations would also greatly benefit such districts as Basford. In Nottingham the station proposed would be much nearer to the lace warehouses than the present station.

Mr. Edward Goldschmidt, the then deputy mayor, Mr. T. Acton, Mr. B. Steibel, past President of the Chamber of Commerce, Mr. Malcolm, and Mr. Robert Mellors gave similar testimony in favour of the Bill, together with the Right Hon. J. W. Mellor, Q.C., who explained the difficulties under which Ruddington laboured by reason of the lack of railway accommodation. The new line would not only be of enormous convenience to Nottingham, but to places like Ruddington and to similar surrounding districts.

Witnesses were afterwards called as to the attitude of East Leake, Hucknall Torkard, Loughborough, Leicester, Chesterfield, Grimsby, and other places affected by the scheme.

This was followed by the important evidence of Mr. Pollitt, general manager of the Great Central Railway, who traced the development of Grimsby, upon whose dock works the company had expended £2,341,000, irrespective of £300,000 on the company's fleet of steamers, the taking over of the South Yorkshire Railway, and dwelt upon the difficulties and losses under which the company laboured by the lack of through connections.

At Nottingham, he explained, they proposed to be in the very centre of town with their stations. When they met the Nottingham people with regard to the railway sanctioned in 1889 they said it was not what they wanted, but they would support it as giving them something, and the hope of their having a further extension right through the town. What they wanted was a company running through the town southwards, and a central station, and they gave the company clearly to understand that they would not be satisfied with the Great Central line until it was carried into the town.

He believed that the new trunk line would greatly strengthen the position of the company financially, and that the new line, within a moderate period, would exceed the existing line in its earning powers, and the main factor in achieving that end would be the large traffic that they at that time dealt with throughout the whole system, the larger traffic they would get when the new line was constructed in Derbyshire and Notts., the new traffic they would secure from Yorkshire to London and through the north-eastern district, and the very considerable traffic they would be able to carry between the large centres of population, such as Nottingham, Leicester, &c., through which the line was to run.

One of the council for those objecting to the Bill tried to make capital out of the suggestion that the Great Central did not know what they were going to spend upon the undertaking, but Mr. Pollitt's reply that they had something more than ideas was terse and to the point.

With regard to the London section of the scheme the company had no slight difficulty to surmount in relation to the Marylebone Cricket Club ground, but this was happily overcome upon the basis of an agreement which was acceptable to both parties. The objection strongly urged by residents of St. John's Wood to the interference which the railway would entail in regard to the quiet residential character of the neighbourhood was also a matter about which a great deal was said. In support of the objection upon this score many witnesses were called, including Mr. Boulnois, M.P., the Rev. Canon Duckworth (vicar of St. Mark's, St. John's Wood), Mr. Briton Riviere, A. R. A. , and others, who contended that the railway would entirely alter the character of the neighbourhood. As president of the Society for the Preservation of Open Spaces, Mr. G. Shaw-Lefevre, M.P., formulated an objection against the proposed terminus being in St. John's Wood. Sir J. Whitaker Ellis, M.P., gave evidence in opposition on behalf of the Maryon Wilson Estate. Another important witness was Lord Grimsthorpe, who spoke as to the effect the proposed railway would have upon the property of the Clergy Orphan Corporation in St. John's Wood, and in a variety of private interests other evidence was given.

In support of the petition of the Midland Railway Company, Mr. Macdonald, engineer, and Mr. G. H. Turner, general manager, were called, whilst Sir Henry Oakley, on behalf of the Great Northern Company, gave further evidence in opposition, stating that the agreement with the Great Central Company would have to come to an end if the new line were sanctioned, and he urged that in the interests of the public it was better the agreement should be continued.

It was a testimony to the excellent scheme of the engineers concerned that such eminent witnesses as Sir George Bruce and Sir Frederick Bramwell, testified to the Committee their belief that the plans had been most skilfully arranged.

After an exhaustive inquiry, which terminated on June 16th., the Chairman announced that the preamble of the Bill was not proved. The decision created a great amount of surprise, and in no quarter was the disappointment more keenly felt probably than in Nottingham. So strong was the feeling that there was a proposal in favour of moving a re-committal of the Bill, but nothing came of this, and for the time being the Parliamentary struggle was at an end.

PARLIAMENTARY SANCTION AT LENGTH OBTAINED

Great was the disappointment following upon the rejection of the Bill by the Committee presided over by Mr. Woodall, it was only to be expected that the application would be renewed in the ensuing session of Parliament. Confident in its claims to sanction for the important scheme which has now been completed, the company made its second application in the session of 1892. The Bill was then relegated to the consideration of a Committee, which was presided over by Sir Richard Paget, who had as his colleagues Mr. Leverson-Gower, Mr. Grotrian, and Mr. Rowntree.

Although to a large extent in the course of the enquiry much of the old ground was traversed, many new features as strengthening elements in the case were presented for consideration. Councel representing the applicants suggested in the course of his opening statement that the very existence of lines running through manufacturing centres must inevitably develop the traffic of the districts through which they passed. The view of the company was that the time had arrived when, in the public interest, it was extremely desirable to form another railway.

The details of the scheme were enumerated, and it was contended that the value which Nottingham and other towns attached to the establishment of the line and stations in their midst was incalculable. It was pointed out that there was a large tract of undeveloped country between Nottingham and Loughborough, and all along the line the one cry was that the villages were getting deserted, and this it was most desirable to arrest. The promoters urged that nothing would bring this about so much as the railway they proposed to provide.

The wish of Leicester was that they should have a better accommodation, and the Bill was supported by the local authorities, and, in fact, by everybody in the borough. No sooner was the previous year's Bill thrown out than in every one of the principal towns resolutions were passed by Chambers of Commerce and other public organisations begging the promoters to repeat their application. Feeling was unanimous in favour of the Bill. The population of the district along the proposed line was then 481,000, and the public bodies in favour of the measure were those of Nottingham, Sheffield, Leicester, Wakefield, Leeds and Barnsley. There were 117 petitions asking that the scheme might be approved.

In the previous year the Great Northern Company were strenuous opponents, on the ground that the promoters wished to break an agreement that had long existed, but that had been rearranged, and they were as satisfied as anybody of the reasonable demand which was made. It was suggested that no stronger evidence in favour of the line could be adduced than that the Great Northern had dropped its opposition and had become a supporter of the Bill.

The Midland Railway did not appear to oppose, and the opposition of the London and North-Western Company was confined to some minor questions of detail as to the construction of the end of the line.

The promoters asked the Committee not to let the opposition of a few people at each end of the proposed new line stand in the way of the construction of the railway, which it was firmly maintained would be of the greatest possible advantage to the fish trade of Grimsby, to the colliery industries of South Yorkshire, to the agricultural community whose districts would be traversed by the line, and to all the great centres of manufacture, which would come within its range. It was urged that the Great Central had done more for the districts which it served than any of the companies which entered into competition with it, but it had never derived the advantages it ought to have done for the simple reason that it only had a short run before it was compelled to pass the traffic over into the hands of its competitors. The company now proposed to expend six millions upon a railway which they were convinced would be a great success.

A very large number of witnesses were called in substantiation of the application, it being suggested that the scheme was bolder, and an improvement upon the one submitted previously. The shareholders without a dissentient voice approved of the Bill, as did also the Board. It was urged that if the extension was authorised and carried into effect it would not prejudice the interests of the Midland Railway Company.

Among the witnesses called was the then Mayor of Nottingham, Mr. R. Fitzhugh, who expressed the opinion that the scheme would be beneficial to the town generally. In addition to the advantages which the Central Station would be, the line opened up a new route to Ruddington and Loughborough, a district to a great extent without railway accommodation, and it would also, he thought, considerably develop the mineral resources in other parts. Sir Samuel George Johnson (Town Clerk) was another of the chief witnesses in support of the Bill.

With reference to the 29 millions representing the capital of the company, it was explained by Mr. Pollitt, that the greater portion of the money expended in railways for the benefit of the great coal fields. The proposed line was to be extended through Nottingham, by the direct invitation of the Corporation. In relation to the revenue it was estimated that the annual earnings on the existing trunk line of the Great Central was £12,000 per mile, the average being £11,000 per mile per annum. Earnings of that kind would give them over the whole of the then existing and the proposed line, a total income of £1,078,000 per annum, and after deducting for working expenses it was calculated that there would be a dividend 6.69 per cent. No doubt whatever was entertained but that in the event of the scheme being authorised the capital required for construction of the works would be easily raised. Since the applicants were last before Parliament, one and a half millions of capital at 4 per cent. had been raised.

The opposition was eventually reduced to almost purely metropolitan objections, a strong protest again being raised to the introduction of the line into St. John's Wood and other parts of that neighbourhood.

At the conclusion of the enquiry, which extended over a period of 22 days, the Committee found the preamble of the Bill proved.

CUTTING OF THE FIRST SOD

It was on November 13th., 1894, that the first sod of the London end of the line was cut, the ceremony being performed by Lady Wharncliffe. Upon that occasion at Alpha-road there was a gathering which will remain memorable in the history of the undertaking. It fell to Sir Edward Watkin, the predecessor of Lord Wharncliffe in the chairmanship of the company, to ask Lady Wharncliffe's acceptance of the wheelbarrow and spade with which to perform the ceremony, and in response to the hearty thanks which were then tendered, Lord Wharncliffe recalled the interesting circumstances that it was so long ago as 1864 that he first became a director of the company. Lord Wharncliffe frankly admitted that when the idea of the new line was mooted he was not struck with the notion, and even in his most sanguine mood he had not expected to live to see the realisation of the project.

At the subsequent banquet which was held at the Holborn Restaurant, Lord George Hamilton proposed the toast of the day - "Success to the new London line."

Having regard to the history of the undertaking, his lordship significantly observed that only those who were in the first rank of railway management, or those distinguished legal men who conducted great railway Bills through Committees of the House of Commons and the House of Lords, had any conception of the difficulties which attended any attempt of any railroad trying to get access to its own capital. It was in accordance with the facts as Lord George Hamilton stated that owing to the multiplicity of interests touched by any great railway enterprise attempting to connect the provinces with London, the approach had to be fought inch by inch by the company attempting to obtain its purpose, more in the manner of a general in a hostile country than a peaceful company trying to get to the capital of its own country.

Those who know most about the vicissitudes of the Great Central Company can well appreciate the statement which was made by the present Secretary of State for India. Indomitable energy, tenacity, and ability of purpose was the phrase employed by Lord George Hamilton with regard to the services of Sir Edward Watkin in connection with the company.

Lord George Hamilton appositely added that the scene which the ceremony had witnessed was appropriately termed Alpha. That the company would obtain the Omega of their troubles was the speaker's ardently expressed wish which now finds practical exemplification in the possibility of the travelling public using the new artery of communication between the North and South.

Upon the occasion mentioned Lord Wharncliffe explained that the reasons for their action in following the examples of other railway companies in England in extending their line and getting to London were very simple. In the first place there was the small proportion of the mileage they got out of the traffic consigned to them. Figures prepared by Mr. Pollitt showed that out of the gross receipts for coaching they received only 35.52 per cent., and other lines 64.48 per cent.; out of the merchandise 41.29 per cent., and other lines 58.71 per cent.; out of coal 24.01 per cent., and other lines 75.99 per cent.; out of fish 40.89 per cent., and other lines 59.11 per cent. These showed that on the whole they averaged only 33.36 per cent., whilst other lines took 66.64 per cent. Therefore out of traffic put on their lines they received very little of the whole.

Another suggestion he laid before them was the great advantage which had accrued to other railways from spending money in extensions. The Midland increased their percentage of capital by 102 per cent., or more than double, and in return they had received in increased revenue an additional 117 per cent. The Great Western had increased their expenditure by 77.34 per cent., and the return in revenue had been an increase by 95.35 per cent. The Manchester, Sheffield and Lincolnshire had increased their capital by 79 per cent., and their increase in revenue had been 99.2 per cent. extra. That proved, he contended, that the policy of the Board, although they had spent such a large sum of money, was a good one, and the returns showed they were justified in launching out as they had done.

There was another reason why they were justified in extending to London, and that was that the increased population was such that there was ample room for another line. Within a radius of 15 miles from Charing Cross the population had increased 45 per cent. in 20 years; for whereas in 1871 the population was 3,885,600, it was 5,637,000 in 1891.

As has been already explained, the original idea in relation to the extension was to work from Quainton-road to London in conjunction with the Metropolitan Company but serious differences, which have recently arisen between the two bodies, have led to the determination to affect a coalition with the Great Eastern Company. Jointly with the Great Central the Company is promoting a Bill to enable them to become part owners with the Great Central Company of a portion of railway, authority to construct which was given by an Act of 1897, and by means of which a junction may be effected near Northolt. The line when constructed is to run to High Wycombe, near which place it will join the existing railway of the Great Western Company running from High Wycombe to Prince's Risborough, a distance of eight miles. It is proposed to double this railway, and to effect improvements in the gradients and curves. The intention is to construct from Prince's Risborough Junction, northward, a line jointly with the Great Western to a point near Grendon-Underwood, where it will join the Great Central new line to London.

As was explained by Lord Wharncliffe at the last meeting of the Great Central Company, the construction of these lines, if authorised, will give the Great Central a new and much better route to London than by running over the existing Metropolitan Railway. The distance will be increased, but this will be more than counterbalanced by the better gradients and curves of the new line.

FROM ANNESLEY TO NOTTINGHAM

Annesley forms the starting point of the Great Central Railway Company's extension to London, and it so happens that at its very commencement the undertaking provides an illustration of the beneficent effect which it can scarcely fail to have upon the company's fortunes. It was at Annesley that the Manchester, Sheffield, and Lincolnshire Company were, in former times, compelled to hand over to neighbours all that extensive mineral traffic which by their own enterprise they had secured, and it is not inappropriate that the colliery village should now become the point at which the newly named company assumes its own responsibilities and commences to reap its own harvest.

From the passenger's point of view Annesley hardly enters into the prospect of future development, but it possesses great possibilities as the centre of a thriving trade in coal even more profitable than the carriage of the ever-increasing multitude of railway travellers. Heavy goods traffic from the North, and the rich output of the coalfields, which the Great Central Company have been accustomed to transfer to the Great Northern for conveyance to Nottingham and the South, will now pass along the Central Company's own lines, and arrangements for collecting and sorting it at Annesley are upon the most complete and elaborate scale. Thus early in its construction the extension to London bears evidence of the thoroughness and care which have been bestowed upon it throughout its entire length, and it is but bare justice to allow that in its every detail the new line worthily ranks with those which have preceded it by many years in "the race to the Metropolis".

Under the guidance of skilful and experienced engineers, coupled with the efficient and loyal assistance of contracting firms of high repute, the Great Central Company have carried out their gigantic scheme with unbounded success. Other articles will deal with the work along the entire route to London; it is the purpose of the present to describe the operations along that section which lies between Annesley and the northern end of the city of Nottingham, a distance of ten miles.

Along the whole of this length the engineer-in-chief has been Mr. Edward Parry, of Nottingham, who upon the inauguration of the undertaking was entrusted with the responsible task of supervising the work from Annesley to Rugby, and the contractors for the first twenty miles - i.e., to East Leake - were Messrs. Logan and Hemingway. While encountering no obstacles of special difficulties in their progress from Annesley to the city, engineers and contractors alike were called upon to execute work of considerable magnitude, and of no less interest, and its principal features were the immense gravitation sidings at Annesley, the removal of a vast amount of rock in a cutting north of Hucknall Town Station, the erection of an imposing viaduct at Bulwell, and extensive tunnelling within the confines of Nottingham. The result of their labours has met with approbation on every hand.

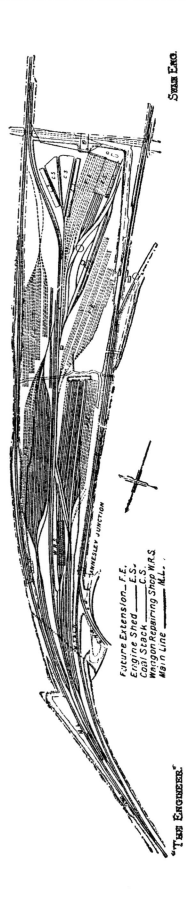

ANNESLEY SIDINGS

Future Extension_F.E.
Engine Shed ———— E.S.
Coal Stack ———— C.S.
Waggon Repairing Shop W.R.S
Main Line ———— M.L.

ANNESLEY JUNCTION

SWAN ENG.

"THE ENGINEER."

Along the stretch of main line from Annesley to Nottingham 31 bridges and one aqueduct have been erected, and there are four bridges on branch lines. Embankments number eleven and cuttings thirteen, and the Sherwood-rise and Mansfield-road tunnels are 668 and 1,200 yards long respectively. For a distance of six miles, from Annesley to Bulwell, the line falls at an average rate of 1 in 132, and after a short piece of level it rises 1 in 330 for about three-quarters of a mile. Then there is another half-mile level, and at 7¼ miles south of Annesley the line resumes the ruling gradient to the Central Station. Through stations the gradient, as a rule, is 1 in 200, but at Carrington it is 1 in 264.

Figures are oftentimes regarded as dull and uninteresting, but it gives some idea of the magnitude of the work carried out within a comfortable radius of the city when it is stated that from cuttings on the main line no fewer than 928,000 cubic yards of earth were excavated, this amount being considerably augmented by the addition of 259,500 cubic yards taken out at Annesley sidings, and 43,000 cubic yards for the Haydn-road carriage sidings. The embankments over the same distance contain 1,280,000 cubic yards of material, and it is interesting to note that the highest bank is that which crosses the valley of the Day Brook, 54ft., while the deepest cutting, 70ft., is situated at the north end of Sherwood-rise tunnel.

Work on the section under notice was commenced on October 16th., 1894, by the sinking of the first shaft in Sherwood-rise tunnel, and it has been prosecuted with very little interruption, the weather for the most part having proved extremely favourable. Up till this period the Great Central Company had their own line up to a point some 400 yards from the Annesley tunnel, herefrom they were compelled to run into Nottingham over the rails of the Great Northern Company. It is at this point, now known as the Annesley junction, that the extension to London actually begins, and just opposite the junction a huge water tower, with a holding capacity of 100,000 gallons, or 450 tons, has been erected. The supply is drawn from the tunnel, and it is amply sufficient to serve the adjacent sidings.

To afford accommodation for their extensive works at Annesley the company found it necessary to purchase upwards of 65 acres of land, and these have now been transformed into a perfect network of rails, together with the engine shed and waggon repairing shops, and other buildings indispensable to the efficient equipment of the sidings.

The up and down main lines upon leaving the tunnel bear away to the east beyond the first signal cabin on the extension, and are kept quite distinct from the goods loop sidings. The latter are rather more than a mile in length, and their northern end is about ten chains south of the junction. On the east side of the goods loop, which runs straight through the centre, lie the up-reception sidings, which can accommodate 190 waggons, while the down-reception sidings, with capacity for 225 waggons, are on the west side. Both sets of sidings eventually run into their respective departure sidings close to the waggon repairing shop. The departure sidings for the North have a capacity for 600 waggons, while those for the South will accommodate 650.

LINBY BRIDGE, OVER THE G.N.R.

The gradient of the reception sidings is 1 in 80, and that of the departure sidings 1 in 132, both sets falling southwards.

The up-departure sidings rejoin the goods loop at a distance of three-quarters of a mile from the junction, and at this point the roads communicating with the engine shed, coal stage, &c., leave it on the west. The goods loop is continued to a point just beyond the drive to Newstead Abbey, where it becomes merged once again in the main lines. A signal cabin is located at each end of the sidings, and there are four smaller cabins to deal with the traffic in the sidings themselves.

The waggon repairing shop has accommodation for 50 waggons. It is an exceedingly well-lighted and admirably arranged building, with a lathe shop, smithy, timber store, and rooms for inspectors and shunters. Fitted with the most improved machinery, it provides every facility for repairing all kinds of damage, whether slight or extensive. In close proximity to Newstead Station on the Great Northern Railway there is a building still in course of erection, in which it is intended to house a plant for generating the electricity which is to be utilised to light the sidings.

Adjoining the engine shed the contractors have erected some buildings for the engine-drivers, and within easy distance are located a smaller water tower, the coal stage, the sand-drying furnace, and the turn-table. The engine shed has a somewhat imposing frontage to the north, and a large clock, visible from all parts of the sidings, has been erected. The shed which measures 180 ft. by 210 ft., contains six lines of rails, and a capacity for 30 engines. Roomy offices are provided for the foreman and the clerks, and along the west side are situated the smithy, pumping and engine rooms, and other apartments for storage purposes.

When our representative paid a visit to Annesley recently a number of the new third-class carriages which the Great Central Company intend to use on their great undertaking were being housed in the engine shed. They are cosily furnished, fitted with steam-heating apparatus, and with the electrical communicator for the guard and engine driver. Each carriage bears the new coat-of-arms of the company, an appropriate and effective design, with the motto "Forward." All the paraphernalia inseparable from the work of the break-down gang are also located in the engine shed.

Outside the shed ample space is left for future extension, and in view of the disastrous results of the coal strike in 1893 the company have also made provision for storing a huge stock of coal, a precaution adopted in many other instances along the line of the route.

The main lines are carried over the drive to Newstead Abbey by means of a handsome stone bridge, somewhat more in keeping with the romantic associations of the neighbourhood than the accustomed structures of steel and brick, and the signal cabin which controls the entrance to and exit from the goods loop at the same spot is also built of dressed stone.

Between Annesley and Hucknall the new line traverses an embankment of moderate height, and in its course crosses the Great Northern and Midland Company's lines at Linby, on massive steel girder bridges. That over the

CUTTING AT HUCKNALL

Great Northern line is of special design, the girders being carried on rollers to allow for expansion and contraction, frequently caused by climatic conditions. The girders in the centre of the three spans are 88ft. long. The bridge over the Midland Railway is also one of three spans, two of them being 40ft. on the square, and the other 61ft. on the skew.

Nearing Hucknall the embankment ceases, and the line runs under the level of several new streets, the laying out of which has necessitated the erection of a lofty retaining wall. The Annesley road is carried over by means of a massive girder bridge, and at Washdyke-lane there is another bridge, composed of steel girders and jack arches, while an aqueduct serves to carry a small stream over the rails. At this point the Hucknall cutting is reached. The contractors here found themselves confronted by a vast mass of magnesian limestone rock, which was exceedingly obstinate, and occupied many months in excavation. So hard was the formation indeed, that steam drills and 2lb. charges of gelignite had to be constantly employed in its removal. The cutting is upwards of a mile in length with a maximum depth of 36ft. and the total excavations amounted to 270,000 cubic yards.

Hucknall Town Station, the first on the extension, is situated just to the south of the cutting. The island platform system is adopted here, as in almost every other instance, and the booking offices are located to the east of a massive bridge on the Watnall-road, from which the station is reached by means of a covered gangway and staircase. The station buildings are conveniently arranged, and admirably lighted, and ample provision has been made further siding accommodation.

A branch line of 250 yards length to the Hucknall Colliery Company's pits leaves the main at a short distance from the station, and the latter then traverses one of the biggest embankments on the section until it reaches Bulwell viaduct, a massive structure, which has elicited general admiration. Four hundred and fifteen yards long, it contains no fewer than 25 arches and one steel span. Five of the arches over the Midland Railway Company's Nottingham to Mansfield line are built on the skew, and at its highest point the viaduct is 68ft. from foundation to parapet.

At a distance of about a quarter of a mile from the Bulwell Common Station there is a flying junction with the Great Northern Company's Leen Valley Railway at Bestwood Park intended chiefly for mineral traffic. Bulwell Common Station is built upon much the same plan as that at Hucknall, except that the booking office is situated on the platform, and a number of new roads to the west afford ample and convenient means of access.

The agreement between the G. C. R. and the G. N. R. which led up to the joint use of the Nottingham Central Station has brought in its train the necessity to construct several additional junctions between the two companies for an interchange of passenger traffic to the north as well as to the south of the city. The first of the number leaves the G. C. R. main line some few hundred yards from Bulwell station, and connects up with the Basford and Bulwell station on the G. N. system from Nottingham to Derby. Beyond this branch the new extension runs through a cutting, and having crossed the

HUCKNALL STATION

G. N. Derby line, reaches the embankment across the valley of the Day Brook, which carries it down to the New Basford (Haydn-road) station.

In the course of this embankment another junction with the neighbouring company's Basford and Bulwell Station is effected. Trains from the latter can, in future, leave the Great Northern line on the north, and running down a decline pass under the metals of both companies, and rise, on a steep gradient to the east of the Day Brook embankment, while traffic from the Nottingham Central Station may leave the same embankment at a point to be known as Bagthorpe Junction, and travel in a westerly direction from the Great Central Railway to Basford Station. In this way the Great Northern route to Derby will be considerably shortened, while greater facilities are afforded for travelling to and from London on the Great Central Railway, to residents in the Erewash Valley.

North of New Basford Station a large plot of land was purchased to accommodate the oil-gas works, and a carriage shed, which are now all but completed. The carriage shed is 300ft. long by 80ft. wide, and contains six sets of rails. The roof is of corrugated iron and glass, and every device to facilitate the cleaning of the carriages has been provided. The shed is heated by steam, passing through pipes which traverse course of the six pits under each set of rails, and lighted by gas. The oil-gas works embrace condenser, boiler, and retort houses, with ample storage, and a gasometer having communication with the carriage shed. Pope's system is to be adopted, and the special trucks which are to convey gas to other lighting stations will, it is expected, be filled at these works.

New Basford Station is approached by a covered staircase from Haydn-road over which the line is carried on a double bridge. Leaving the station trains from the North run through a short, but very deep, cutting into the Sherwood-rise tunnel. This has a uniform height of 20ft., and a maximum width of 27ft., and massive walls of sandstone rock, through which the excavator had to pierce, serve as supports to the arched roof.

Carrington Station is located between the Sherwood-rise and Mansfield-road tunnels, and it provides the only instance up to this point in which an island platform has not been provided, while Arkwright-street, on the other side of the Nottingham Central Station, is its only other counterpart on the whole extension to London. The booking office and the stationmaster's house at Carrington face the Gregory-boulevard, and the up platform can be reached therefrom by a sloping path, while those who desire to travel north cross the metals by means of a footbridge.

The Mansfield-road tunnel, with its extreme length of 1,200 yards may be regarded a typical example of the care and exactitude which have been exercised by both engineers and contractors along the section. Unlike that which passes under Sherwood-rise, it contains three pronounced curves, and yet the headings were driven with such accuracy from the three shafts that there was not a deviation even of a few inches from the exact route traced out upon the surface. At the deepest point the rails are 100 feet below street level, but such was the character of the rock that the contractors were able to

BULWELL VIADUCT

CARRINGTON STATION

ROUTE THROUGH THE CITY

dispense almost entirely with sides. The exception occurs at the Gregory-boulevard end, where the work was of a somewhat delicate character. Boring and bricking had to be carried out here in much shorter lengths owing to the slight depth below the road level, and the artificial supports are of a far more substantial character than was necessary in any other portion of the tunnel. The roof has a uniform height throughout of 20ft. above the rails, and from the springing of the arches on the rock sides to the crown there is a measurement of 8ft. 6in., leaving a wall of rock on either side 13ft. 6in. in height. The arches are faced with 18 inches of blue brick and the actual width of the tunnel between the rock sides is 27ft., or 29ft. between the springing of the arches.

A number of manholes are provided for the use of platelayers, together with a larger recess 10ft. square, at each end to serve as storehouses, and a 12in. drain for carrying sewage from Carrington Station. The southern face of the tunnel is just below the junction of the Woodborough-road and Windsor-street, where the site of the Central Station commences in a cutting 60ft. deep.

Readers will have gathered that travelling northwards from Nottingham there is a long, steady, pull to Annesley, and it is interesting to note that while the Central Station is 110ft. above the level of the sea, Annesley sidings are 332ft. higher. Between Annesley and Rugby the lowest point is at Ruddington, 91ft. above the level of the sea, and the highest at Lutterworth, 445ft.

Under Mr. Parry's supervision the work has been expeditiously and efficiently accomplished. He has had the assistance of a capable and courteous staff, to whom we are indebted for the facilities afforded to obtain information. The map showing the route to London and the plan of Annesley sidings are reproduced by permission of The Engineer.

In the preceding article dealing with the Great Central Railway extension the course of the new line was traced from Annesley to the Nottingham station site. The work at the latter point has been one of the most important in relation to the undertaking, and it has presented many engineering features of special interest. No greater transformation has been effected in any other part. The plan which we publish to-day indicates the route through the city with the various contiguous thoroughfares, the site covered by the new station also being shown by the dotted lines. The whole character of no small portion of the city has been completely changed, and in the place of several well known landmarks, and it must be confessed, of much property of a not very desirable class, a structure has sprung up which is a credit to the companies concerned in its erection, and which the citizens of Nottingham can with some amount of pride congratulate themselves upon having in their midst.

It may not be uninteresting at this stage to mention some of the alterations which have taken place almost in the heart of the town as a result of the undertaking. Charlotte-street, Mount East-street, Brunswick-street, Sherwood-lane, Lamb-lane, St. George's-square, Barrett's and many other yards, as well as numerous courts, have entirely disappeared. Portions of

NOTTINGHAM CENTRAL STATION DURING CONSTRUCTION

Milton-street and Mansfield-road have been demolished, and nearly the whole of Cairns-street has been done away with. Little has been left of Newcastle-street, whilst the bottom end of York-street, the west end of St. Ann's-street, and the west end of William-street have also been pulled down. In other words, all the buildings from a point at the west end of Woodborough-road, as far as Lower Parliament-street, bounded on the west side by property facing Mansfield-road (up to a spot nearly fronting Shakespeare-street), and Milton-street (from opposite Burton-street), and roughly speaking on the east, over-looked by Windsor-street and Glasshouse-street, have been swept away.

The chief structures involved in the clearance have been St. Stephen's Church and Schools, the Union Workhouse, the Ragged School in Newcastle-street, a block of slaughter-houses in Cairns-street, and a number of public-houses, amongst them being the Shakespeare and Plough and Harrow Inns, the Duke of York Inn, and the Bird in Hand beerhouse, York-street, and the Queen Caroline Inn, Charlotte-street.

The whole area of the site is 12 acres. From Woodborough-road to Thurland-street is a distance of three-eighths of a mile, otherwise 700 lineal yards, or 2,100 feet. The average width is therefore 83 yards, or 250 feet, the widest point being 390 feet.

As soon as the Great Central Company obtained possession under their Parliamentary powers, they disposed of the various properties in lots, and the work of demolition proceeded apace. The area was fenced in, and the contractors next began operations. What are known as headings were driven and tunnels made, and in a comparatively short period quite a number of steam navvies were at work. The material at the top end lying between Woodborough-road and Charlotte-street was found to be principally rock formation, and it was so hard that gunpowder had to be used to loosen it, but the other portion was comparatively soft, and indications pointed strongly to the fact that at one time there had been a valley running parallel to Parliament-street, the spot where the channel or watercourse had existed being plainly discernible. From this site material to the extent of 580,000 cubic yards has been removed, the depth of the immense hole as it may now be termed being 58ft. 6in. at the Woodborough-road end and 27ft. at the Parliament-street end. As before stated, no small engineering difficulties were met with.

Deep down nearly in the middle or the site three old cellars were discovered. There was only one entrance to them, forming what may, for the purposes of illustration, be described as a bottle neck, and the excavators had to go right to the bottom of them in order to obtain a foundation for the footbridge. This done the cellars were left in their original state. The old sewer which came across from Charlotte-street had also to be diverted, and this proved an exceedingly arduous piece of work, for it was all underground, and the heading was a very small one. However it has been carried along Milton-street and Parliament-street to Cur-lane. Originally egg-shaped, its form has been retained, except here it passes under the railway lines below the Parliament-street bridge, where it is 5ft. 6in. in diameter.

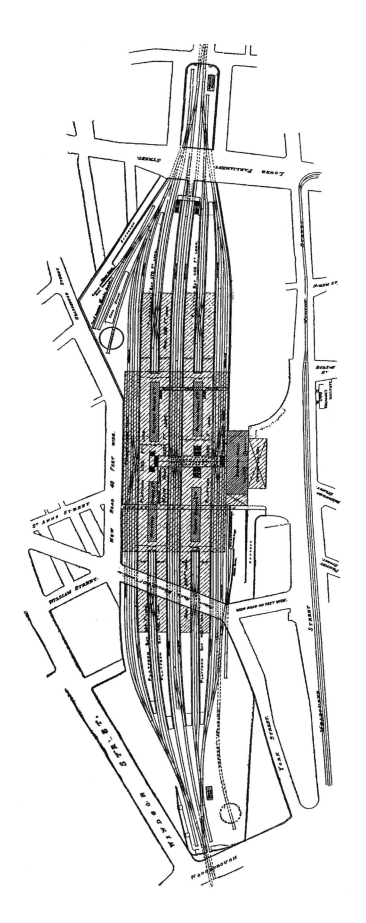

PLAN OF THE NOTTINGHAM STATION

The new station is a splendid structure, and both as regards arrangement and equipment it will compare with every advantage with any in the country. Nearly the whole of the area excavated is covered by the building, which is of course almost completely hidden from view. It is, however, proposed to erect a clock tower in the centre, and this will no doubt be a striking feature, whilst the new hotel it is intended to construct opposite the Mechanics' Institution, may be depended upon to be a building which will add considerably to the appearance of the neighbourhood. The main approach, as is now generally known, is almost opposite Shakespeare-street. The width of Mansfield-road at that point as well as opposite the Mechanics' Institution and the Baptist Church has been extended to 130ft., and it provides most suitable means of access.

There will be a covered cabway immediately in front of the booking-hall, to which entrance is first gained. This will be erected with the floor on the street level, and will be a spacious room, being about 120ft. long by nearly 70ft. wide. It will contain offices for the use of both the Great Central Company and the Great Northern Company. On the right hand side is a cloak-room, 45ft. by 55ft., whilst on the left are parcels offices 85ft. by 70ft., the latter being built on girders. From this place passengers proceed to a foot-bridge, from which they descend to the platforms.

As is shown in the accompanying plan there are two magnificent island platforms, the term island being aptly used for the reason that there are sets of rails on each side. Trains can, of course, draw up on each side of the two "islands", and there are thus four platforms which vary in length from nearly 1,200ft. to 1,270ft. The lines running through the centre will be used for the main up and down passenger traffic, there being a spare road between them. Goods trains will pass through on each extreme side of the station. At each end of the island platforms bays have been inserted. Two lines of rails run into all the four, and trains can thus draw up at eight additional platforms in these places, the average length being about 400ft. All are admirably finished.

From the coping to the foundation wall beneath is a space of a foot, to allow for signal rods, &c., the coping stone being adamantine in character, and all the ends are made complete by ramps or declines, the fall being 1 in 8, so as to enable porters and other officials to easily reach the permanent way. It will thus be seen that the accommodation for all kinds of traffic is exceedingly great. Handsome blocks of buildings, in which are waiting and refreshment rooms, offices, and all the conveniences of a first-class station, have been erected in the central portion. The exterior of these establishments is buff glazed brickwork with terra cotta facing, those above being semi-circular, whilst the top ones are segmentary with terra cotta moulds and cornices.

The structures rise to a lofty height. As a matter of fact, the steel columns supporting the roof rise 42ft. 6in. above the platform level, some of the columns giving a span of 30ft., and others a short one of 15ft. The roof is 450ft. long, and it goes over in fine spans from a screen wall faced with glazed white bricks on the Mansfield-road side to a similar one on the Glasshouse-street boundary. Apart from the main roof the framework of which is of braced steel, there are prettily-constructed awnings over all the bays, and passengers are, therefore, never likely to suffer from the inclemency of the weather.

An excellent system of subways has been carried out. One follows the route of the passenger footbridge from the booking hall, and being 14ft. wide and 11ft. 2in. high luggage can easily be conveyed along it. Others encircle the central building blocks, and, all being connected, their utility, particularly in connection with the dining-room arrangements, will be exceedingly great. There are, too, fitted with hydraulic lifts. Room has been found in them for the drainage pipes from the station, which are carried to the sewer in Parliament-street. That the construction of these subways was a rather costly matter will be readily understood when it is mentioned that in many cases they had to be cut out of the solid rock, and that they are lined with brick work, the arches being glazed. All the other appointments of an important station have been provided.

There are signal boxes fitted up with the most modern arrangements at the north and south ends, where the rails in each case form a perfect network. The lines run into each other in bewildering fashion, and the form of the station has been likened to a bottle at each end. At the corner adjoining Woodborough-road and York-street a large water tank is being erected. Its capacity will be 65ft. by 30ft., and there will be 12 inch mains from it in order to supply all the water columns, the hydraulic buildings, and other places, the supply for all purposes coming from this source. The hydraulic chamber arrangements will be under the bay of the York-street bridge, and from that point to the tank plenty of room remains for future extension.

Behind the detached block of buildings in Mansfield-road, opposite Peachy-street, are horse and carriage docks, and conveniences for the loading and unloading of fish and general market goods. The approach runs down to the left from the main entrance, the incline being 1 in 14, and it curves round to the right and runs under the booking hall. In the corresponding corner, on the Glasshouse-street side, are more carriage, horse, and loading docks. There are also coal stages and an engine turn-table, which can be worked by either hydraulic or hand power. The approach in this case is direct from Parliament-street, the roadway being built on arches so that it will be seen that every possible use has been made of the space at disposal. These arches are noticeable from the fact that the wall within curves backwards, this having been done so that they may bear the pressure of the roadway. The retaining walls of the whole enclosure generally form features of the greatest interest.

It was found unnecessary to build any both on the Mansfield-road and the Windsor-street sides of the Mansfield-road tunnel, the rock being so hard. A parapet, however, has had to be erected near Windsor-street and Woodborough-road, and as it approaches rather near to the cutting the top soil was taken away and the wall built up from the rock. Between Cairns-street and Parliament-street and from Bywell-street to Parliament-street there are other high retaining walls of blue or brindle brick, the one first indicated going to a height of 53ft.

One with recesses in it was necessary for the bay forming the approach to the new York-street bridge. This a massive and imposing structure, crossing the complete set of lines on the north side mortified from Bywell-street to the new roads which have been made and to Glasshouse-street. It is built upon the skew, and has an extreme length of 279ft. The roadway across it is 40ft. wide, and the height from the rail level to that of the road is nearly 30ft. on the east side and 32ft. on the west. It is supported by four rows, there being five steel stanchions in each row. These are fixed to brickwork, and hold-down bolts carry the columns down to the solid rock. They are braced at the top, and longitudinal girders also brace them the other way.

Just under the footpath on the south side is a pipe chamber, through which water, gas, or other pipes can at any time be carried. On the west or York-street side the approach is fan shaped, and it has been made so the more readily to accommodate traffic from York-street and Bywell-street.

To the left of the main entrance to the station is a public footbridge, which goes straight into the new 40ft. roadway running into Glasshouse-street, almost directly opposite St. Ann's-street. It is built of iron, and is 15ft. wide, being carried across on substantial columns. There is a connection with the station passenger footbridge, and there will thus be a convenient outlet for many people. There is another entrance to the station by means of a footbridge from the Parliament-street bridge, the ways from which branch outwards to each of the main platforms. In all respects the station appears complete, and the whole arrangements reflect the highest credit on the designers.

JUNCTION OF THE GREAT CENTRAL AND GREAT NORTHERN LINE
NEAR MALT MILL LANE, NOTTINGHAM

JUNCTION WITH THE GREAT NORTHERN

On the south side the station is bounded by the Parliament-street Bridge. This is another massive structure carrying a roadway nearly 80ft. wide. It is known as a tapering bridge, having a span of about115ft. on the north side, whereas the one on the south is 75ft. There is a narrow gap between the bridge and the entrance to the covered way below Thurland-street. On each side retaining walls of a more substantial description than in any other spot have had to be erected. Owing to the loose nature of the earth the greatest care was necessary in building them, the face of the cutting having to be stoutly propped while the bricks were placed in position. At the bottom of the Parliament-street end the walls are no less than 14ft. 6in. thick, and even at the top they are 7ft. 6in., though this width is not uniform throughout the whole length.

From Thurland-street to Weekday-cross is a covered way or tunnel measuring a distance of 392½ yards. The comparatively slight depth from the rail level to the surface of the streets rendered the labours of the excavators dangerous in the extreme upon this section, and it was not at all an uncommon occurrence to suddenly break through into a rock cellar or some underground apartment. Unusual measures to strengthen the roof whilst the boring proceeded had to be taken. This was, of course, obviated in the first portion, as far as Pelham-street by cutting out to the top, arching and filling up again.

Whilst boring underneath the premises of the Joint Stock Bank in Victoria-street the crown of the arch broke through the basement floor just where the safe was, and as is well known, the company had to buy the building and erect a new one. Further on it was known that some very low cellars would be met with. They were surveyed by Mr. A. A. Barker, one of the engineers upon whom, under Mr. Parry, important work has devolved, and he found that the crown of the tunnel would come right above the floor. Accordingly before any tunnelling at all was done a facsimile of what the arch would be was formed with lime concrete. The whole of the cellaring was then filled in with Portland cement concrete of the best quality, and a new building was erected upon the place. The tunnel was afterwards driven under, perfectly true to the spot, and the lime having been removed the arch was there in its ready state to receive the brickwork.

In the case of the Old Cross Keys Inn, Byard-lane, the men accidentally broke into the rock cellars, and, needless to say, they availed themselves freely to some of the stock-in-trade they found there. The cellars of the Old Dog and Partridge Inn, Parliament-street were met with in a similar manner, but in this case the excavators discovered nothing more than bottles of ginger and herb beer.

The brick arch of the tunnel has been turned from the rock side wall all the distance with the exception of just a little at each end, and much expense in brick work has thus to some extent been spared. For nearly the whole of the

NEW G.N. STATION, LONDON ROAD, NOTTINGHAM

length the crown of the roof is 20ft. from the rail level, but under Victoria-street there is a sudden drop of 3ft. for several yards, owing to the presence above of a large brick sewer. At a distance, too, a manhole has been provided, so that platelayers and others can find safety when trains are passing.

At Weekday-cross the quaint old house celebrated as being the birthplace of Mr. Philip James Bailey, the author of "Festus", had to be demolished, and a new building, on the arch of the tunnel, has been erected. The old Town Hall, with its dungeons and antiquities, had also to disappear, and the tunnel now emerges upon the site it occupied. Garner's-hill runs underneath the line on the skew, Middle-hill has also been altered, and Narrow-marsh has been bridged over.

The Great Northern Company's extension joins the Great Central Company's line at that point. It branches away to the left, and is an important feature in connection with the general scheme, so far as Nottingham is concerned. The junction is on a gradual curve, and is about 20 yards north of the mouth of the tunnel, near to Garner's-hill. At the apex of the junction there is the Weekday-cross signal-box, which practically controls both lines, and contains 20 levers, with provision for more if required.

The whole of the connecting railway has been constructed on viaducts, and near to the bridge which crosses Narrow-marsh is the carting depot of the company, and Messrs. Thompson, McKay, and Co., with stabling built in under the arches. There are several "skew" bridges on the line, all being erected in steel lattice bracings, supplied by the Patent Shaft and Axle Company, of Wednesbury, the firm of Messrs. J. H. and W. Bell, of Liverpool, carrying out the actual work. All the bridges have loose asphalted flooring in order that the rain-water may the more quickly be drained away.

The bridge over Canal-street is a particularly fine one, and here, as in all instances along the line on the bridges, the rails are laid on longitudinal timbers in troughs over steelwork, and between the bridges there is an outside-angle iron guard rail. The sixth of the bridges passes over the Nottingham and Grantham canal, and the line, at this point, runs close behind the premises of the National Telephone Company and the large warehouse of Messrs. Furley and Buttrum.

Near to is the joint station, which is a distinct improvement to the architectural features of the neighbourhood. The building has been furnished with spacious sky lights and the front and interior are of glazed bricks in different colours. In the entrance yard there is ample accommodation for a cab stand, with a shelter. There are four booking offices, together with cloakrooms, parcels office, and accountant's room. From the ground floor there is a luggage lift, and a double flight of steps leads to the platforms above. Here there are four waiting-rooms, the stationmaster's office, porters' room, &c. The length of the platform, which is of "island" shape, is 740 feet, and the pavement is asphalted, with stone copings. The total cost of the works will be about a quarter of a million sterling.

The junction with the Great Northern main line is formed at Meadow-lane; the gradient from Weekday-cross, to the London-road Station is one in 400, and thence to Meadow-lane one in 264 yards. At the gasworks sidings the viaduct is supported by cylinders sunk in the solid rock by the aid of pneumatic pressure, and filled with concrete. There are also new turn-tables fixed, in order to accommodate the goods traffic.

The work has been carried out under the direction of Mr. H. W. Sadler, construction engineer for the Great Northern Company, whose resident representative is Mr. V. B. Hunt; the inspector of works was Mr. Robert Howard, and Mr. C. Pitt has acted as inspector of the steel-work on behalf of the railway company. The old station is not to be abolished, but will be utilised for excess goods and passenger traffic, the junction at Meadow-lane affording easy facilities in this respect.

THE ROUTE THROUGH THE MEADOWS

The fine viaduct which carries the line of the Great Central Company over the Marsh, Canal-street, the Canal, Station-street, the Midland Railway Station and sidings, Queen's-road, and the Meadows, nearly up to the end of Stanley-terrace on the boundary of the old recreation ground, is five-eighths of a mile long, and has in its course 53 arches and 12 steel bridges. The bridges have been constructed with three girders, one being in the centre, so that in the event of anything happening to the others traffic can still be over one line, until repairs have been effected. All the arches are asphalted, the water being collected and conveyed in pipes through the wall. The result is that they are perfectly watertight, and as a consequence their value as storerooms and for stabling and other general purposes has been quickly recognised. The majority are already boarded up and tenanted, and they have become a source of no inconsiderable income to the company.

The actual height of the viaduct from the surface of the ground over which it stretches to rail level varies considerably, but in no case is it less than 16ft. Then from rail level to the top of the parapets, in which are the usual recesses for the protection of platelayers, is about 6ft., so that passengers will not gain much of a view of the district through which they travel.

The viaduct is straight from Weekday-cross to the bridge over Canal-street, and then it curves to the right, all the arches as far as Station-street being on the curve, the span of the one over the Nottingham and Grantham Canal being 45ft. on the square and 48ft. on the skew. The bridge crossing Canal-street is a somewhat peculiar one, the girders on the east side having a length of 69ft., whilst the one on the Carrington-street side is 103ft. long, with a depth at each end of 9ft. 6in., and in the upper part Station-street is crossed by a low girder bridge of 58ft. span, and then comes the great one over the lines of the Midland Company. This has a span of 171ft., and another of 104ft. crosses the sidings. There is cross-bracing to keep the girders in proper position during high winds, and also inner bracing to secure greater firmness. The bridge is indeed of exceptional strength, and there are check rails all along it, as well as over Station-street, to prevent derailment.

The height from the rival company's lines to those of the Great Central Company is 23ft. For the purposes of the great span four enormous cylinders had to be sunk. They were put down in lengths of 4ft. each, and were then bolted together. Their foundation is the sandstone rock, the depth from the surface of the road in one case being 29ft., and in the other 26ft. The work was most trying, owing to water being met with, and pneumatic pressure had inconsequence to be resorted to. Cement concrete and large granite blocks were laid at the bottom, and the stanchions were fastened with hold-down bolts. Some idea of the size and strength of the cylinders may be gathered from the fact that each of the 4ft. lengths weighs 4¾ tons. When properly fixed they were filled in with brickwork and cement.

CROSSING THE NOTTINGHAM MIDLAND STATION

Leaving the Midland Railway, the line again takes a curve of 20 chains radius from Queen's-road to Crocus-street, Arkwright-street, and Waterway-street. These thoroughfares are crossed by very fine bridges and, the line being on the curve, the width between the girders had to be made slightly greater than ordinarily. The placing of the girders in position over Arkwright-street was a most interesting matter. It took 14 horses, the leaders and shaft animals being brought specially from Manchester for the purpose, to draw them from the Great Northern goods yard, and the girders were so long that they were only just able to clear some of the street corners.

Arkwright-street Station is approached from the thoroughfare after which it is named, and immediately adjoins the bridge. The entrance is a commodious one, and contains booking and stationmaster's offices, &c., and flights of steps lead to each platform, there being a passage through one of the arches of the viaduct. Both the platforms are about 425ft. long, and they contain waiting-rooms and other conveniences. They are built out from the viaduct on steel piers, and altogether they are most commodious.

Further on, the viaduct curves to the left to the extent of 60 chains radius. Kirk White-street is crossed, and the Arkwright-street signal box is passed just on the borders of the old recreation ground, and close to Stanley-terrace. The goods yard, with an area of upwards of 35 acres, commences at this point, extending over the new Trent Bridge to the Lovers'-walk, and the line runs on an embankment wide enough to carry four sets of metals, the main passenger road keeping to the left and the one for goods trains to the right, as well as a number of additional lines for shunting purposes.

The goods yard is situated on each side of the permanent way, and is reached by lines which fall in some places on gradients of 1 in 50. Over 650,000 cubic yards of earth have been tipped into the yard, but it still remains 14ft. below the level of the main line. That portion of the yard which lies between the embankment and Queen's-walk is for goods traffic proper, and upon the other side the company have erected several buildings. There is a covered carriage shed 400ft. long and 110ft. wide, with a boiler house for heating purposes, a turn-table for goods engines, and an engine shed 210ft. long by 88ft. wide, capable of holding 16 engines. Plenty of room remains for extending the last-named building, and if required, can be enlarged to accommodate 20 more engines. In addition a coal shed, a tank house, a waggon cover repairing shop, and cattle pens have been constructed, and there are parachute water cranes at both ends.

The cattle pen approach is by means of a road from Ryeland-crescent, in the neighbourhood of which marvellous building changes have been effected. On the site of the old Castle Cricket Club ground, which the company acquired, and far beyond in the direction of the Trent, houses have risen in great numbers. As in the Woodborough-road and Windsor-street district where they erected 125 dwellings for artisans, in order to compensate for those which had been destroyed by their operations, the company have built several large blocks here. The houses number in all 175, and they have been formed in terraces which abut upon Glapton-road.

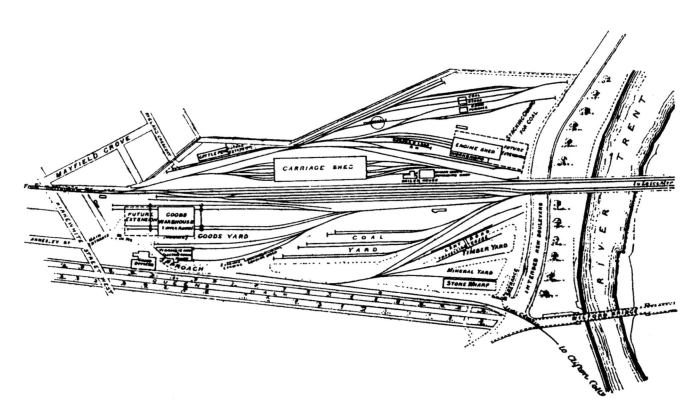

NOTTINGHAM GOODS YARD

It is well-known that the district possesses an unenviable reputation for floods, but the builders have put in solid concrete foundations some little height above the surrounding ground, and the Corporation have made or are making good streets, so that trouble in this respect is likely to be small.

In that portion of the yard situated on the right is the goods warehouse just behind the Queen's-walk police-station and approached from Kirkewhite-street. It is a huge three-storey building with a length of 155ft., and a breadth of 128ft. Four lines of rails run into it, and there is room for two more if required. Carts can also enter the centre bay, and there are numerous hoists and cranes. The centre is opened to the roof, forming a sort of well for hoisting purposes, and the two upper floors all round will be used for storing. At each end are small turn tables, and there is a weighing machine, with an office near to the entrance to the yard.

Further away are goods offices and these are of a very commodious description. There are also hydraulic and electric power houses, engine houses, and loading docks. The coal sidings are extensive, and great conveniences have been made for carting, whilst a Goliath travelling crane, capable of lifting 20 or 30 tons, is in position.

A branch siding has been laid down to Clifton Colliery, and there are other roads from the main lines into the Sidings at the Trent Bridge end, where there is much room for more accommodation. It is intended to have a timber yard about this point, and a strong wharf will in all probability be formed.

Proceeding along the line the bridge which carries it over the Trent is encountered. This is a massive and handsome structure. First of all, there is a span of 66ft. between abutments across the new boulevard, then there are three arch spans of 32ft. 6in. each, and three spans across the river succeed. These latter cover a total length of 325ft., and support four lines of rails, two for the passenger and two for goods traffic. The river spans are carried across on cylinders similar to those upon which the bridge over the Midland railway is built. They were sunk down to the rock under compressed air, and were filled in with Portland cement concrete, and blue bricks in cement mortar. Upon them large granite blocks with holding down bolts were fixed to secure roller bearings to allow for the expansion of the girders. These latter are thoroughly braced, and there are ornamental caps to the columns.

There are seven arches beyond the river, and the full distance from the point at which the viaduct leaves the embankment to that at which it joins the bank on the Wilford side is 861ft., there being 470ft. in the length of abutments, piers, and arches, 66ft. of the boulevard span and 325ft. across the river. The bridge is really a splendid structure, and it is an eloquent tribute to the ability of those who designed and constructed it.

Considerable opposition to it was, it will be remembered, offered by the late Mr. T. Clifton, but there seems no reason to believe that it will in any way affect the Wilford Bridge as he contended would be the case.

The stretch of line from Carrington to Wilford has been constructed under the supervision of Mr. A. A. Barker, who has acted as resident engineer for Mr. Edward Parry, and he and his staff have proved themselves highly capable.

TRENT VIADUCT AT WILFORD

WILFORD TO LOUGHBOROUGH

Although the stretch between Nottingham and Loughborough has not presented exactly those natural difficulties which have been found elsewhere, still it has required unremitting labour on the part of both engineer and contractor to bring the section into unison with the rest of the system. Very generally, the principal feature of the run may be said to lie evenly between the abnormal depth of the cuttings and the great height of the embankments, which follow one upon the other with, what must be to the contractor, satisfactory regularity.

Leaving the splendid constructions which carry the line over the Trent, half a mile to the south of Arkwright-street Station, the route stretches away to the south at a level which practically registers no gradient, and proceeds over the pathway through Wilford fields, crossing on the way what is familiarly known as the "Lovers' Walk" by a bridge of the ordinary steel type, supported by two stout abutments built of ordinary brindle bricks.

About a mile and a half south of the Trent Bridge is a junction and siding constructed for the purpose of accommodating the Wilford Brick Company, which was quite lately, owing in a large measure to the impetus given by the railway, got into full working order. A hundred yards lower down a structure arches an occupation road, used by several neighbouring farmsteads, and a few yards further a third, which serves a similar purpose, has been necessitated. A quarter of a mile away, with the track still lying perfectly level and direct, of practically the same design as those which have preceded it, although of somewhat different proportions, stretches across Wilford road, and 900 yards thence a bridge over a stream is supplemented by flood openings.

A quarter of a mile distant - 12¾ miles from Annesley Junction - the Ruddington-road is carried over the railway by a bridge on the skew, with embanked approaches on either side. It is hereabouts that the first large cutting commences. Passing under the Ruddington-road Bridge the line describes a gradual curve, with but a slight deviation, for having left behind a three arch brick bridge, the principal span of which is about 28 feet, and which has been constructed to accommodate an occupation road, it returns to the absolute straight until a bend is required to enter Ruddington Station.

So far everything has taken the form of a railroad in full working order, and the station erected for the purposes of Ruddington residents bears precisely the same aspect. It is exactly the type of station adopted throughout the whole of the extension. Here we have the island platform, remarkably convenient for passengers, and especially those pressed for time, but fraught with extra responsibility to drivers. The buildings are of bright red brick, and supplied with appointments according to the latest ideas of sanitation and general convenience, with utility.

At the entrance to the station from the highway is the stationmaster's house on the right, with the weighing-machine opposite, and the cattle dock and accommodation for goods traffic favourably located. Already the railway has had a very salutary effect upon the prospects of Ruddington, and when the system is in full working order the people have every hope that it will become a popular residential quarter of the important city of Nottingham.

The island platform is 32ft. wide, and 400ft. in length, and access to the premises is gained by a flight of steps from the road above, leading from a stone arch elevation. The steps are covered with glazed sides and roof, and an ornamental awning offers shelter from the elements, if needs be, until the ticket office, 50 feet away, is attained. To the east of the station there is ample siding accommodation.

Proceeding south, the line resolves itself into a perfectly straight road extending for three and three-quarter miles, the gradually diminishing perspective of which is presented in peculiar telescopic form. The straight commences a little beyond Ruddington, 14 mile 34 chains from the opening of the section, and subsequently a cutting, three-quarters of a mile long, is entered. This has never presented any difficulty to the engineers, and does not exceed in depth 20 feet in any place. A pretty stretch of country is at this point tapped, Gotham, snug among the trees on the one hand, and Bunney, with its hilly surroundings, on the other, affording striking contrast.

Sixteen miles 36 chains below Annesley there is the goods branch to Gotham partially made. It is a single line, about 2½ miles long, running round the village to secure the traffic from several gypsum mines in the vicinity. For an exactly similar distance along the main stretch the line is sustained by an embankment which contains, at a fair estimate, 220,000 cubic yards of material, and at 17 miles 45 chains it dips into a cutting extending only for two chains, and measuring about 10 feet in depth. The break, however, is only momentary, for 60 yards hence the road plunges into another cutting, which rises on either side to about 35 feet, and stretches for close upon half a mile, being spanned en route by a three-arch bridge carrying the road from Gotham to East Leake.

Thirty chains later the line takes a gentle curve, and running along the top of a fine embankment, which has been thrown up for excavations in the last-named cutting, together with that a little further south, sweeps with unbroken front into East Leake Station, having in the meantime widened its embrace to provide spacious sidings. The arrangements here are on the same principle as those at Ruddington - the disposition and character of the buildings being similar, and the only material difference is that entrance to the station is obtained by ascending instead of descending a flight of steps, in consequence of the East Leake to Kegworth road having been diverted and sunk to a level which allows the railway to pass over it. The bridge which supports the line across has been so constructed that by the removal of the brick coping on either side its capacity may be enlarged so as to carry two additional sets of rails.

Without the slightest complexity of crossings and points, as is the case at Ruddington, the main lines here resume their usual parallel connection immediately on leaving the station, and entering the last stretch of Messrs.

Logan and Hemingway's section, run through one of the largest cuttings along the whole extension. At its deepest point it measures 55 feet on the centre line, and almost throughout its length, upwards of half a mile, it seldom deminishes to less than between 30 and 40. From this cutting upwards of 350,000 cubic yards of material have been taken, 31,000 of which were utilised for the last of the embankments, and the remainder was used on the embankment already mentioned on the northerly side of East Leake Station. This was one of the earliest pieces of work to be accomplished, and although there has perforce been some slight slipping, the earthworks have now settled down to comparative solidity, being well drained, "bound" with stone where required, and grass-covered.

A few chains to the south, at a point exactly 19½ miles from Annesley, the Loughborough sub-division of the section is reached, the line of demarcation being most clearly defined, for instead of the light brown Trent gravel which Messrs. Logan and Hemingway have been permitted to use (with a more substantial film on the top), the hard, dark, and sombre Mountsorrel chippings have been employed for ballast by Messrs. Lovatt and Co., of Wolverhampton, whose contract carries the extension onwards to Leicester.

Continuing the journey south, a spot not altogether unknown in the folk lore of the district follows next in order of interesting feature. It is called on the Ordnance Survey Map "The Devil's Garden," but why? No one seems able to tell or even surmise. It is more than probable that in earlier times, when the merest superstition received unaccountable credence, some legend or story of the nursery supplied the tottering foundation for the altogether incongruous name given to a cosy little cover rising abruptly from the railway level. However, this parenthetically; but it is certain that years ago the cover was occasionally "drawn" by the Quorn Hunt before the contractors took part of it away.

Hard by is a short tunnel, measuring 88 yards, which caused a good deal of trouble and some little anxiety to construct, because of the enormous amount of water met with, and the foul gas - in all likelihood marsh gas - that was tapped in the course of operations, necessitating several temporary stoppages. The tunnel is to-day very wet, though absolutely secure. At about the middle of the cutting, which succeeds, a geological "fault" of singular formation was opened out by the steam navvy a few years ago. It had a special charm and interest for the geologists of the district, who have from time to time visited the spot in, comparatively speaking, large numbers.

There is nothing else of a peculiar nature about the cutting, at the southern extremity of which there is a commodious siding put up to receive the traffic from the Barnston Lime Company, well-known dealers in Blue Lias material.

The railway again runs into a deep cutting, 40 feet high in places, and emerges by means of the imposing embankment which carries it along the unbroken sweep of Loughborough meadows. At this point the river Soar is crossed, and what was once a sluggish, tree-grown stream, winding its way carelessly under the side of the hillock, has now an open course and a clean

VIADUCT AND DIVERSION OF THE SOAR, NEAR LOUGHBOROUGH

cut boundary line substantially bricked up as a safeguard against the ravages of flooding. The viaduct, three arches of which bridge the river, is really the finest piece of work on the Nottingham to Loughborough section, and its appearance is enhanced by open approach on either side. The arches which take the river are on the skew, and there are four flood arches to the north and south fixed to the square.

The footway leading across the meadows from Loughborough, skirting Stanford village, and joining the road to Nottingham, has been widened and much improved by the railway authorities, and its course slightly diverted so that the extreme north arch of the viaduct might take it, and speaking generally, the approach to the village of Stanford, not unknown in the annuls of the Quorn Hunt, has been made decidedly more convenient.

The embankment now extends for about a mile, and practically carries the line into the precincts of Loughborough Station at a gradient of 1 in 176, which is the ruling gradient on the whole section. On the way down the Midland Railway (Trent to Leicester) is crossed by means of a fine bridge of four spans, and set on the skew. The superstructure is of steel, with the prevailing blue-brick piers and abutments.

The station at Loughborough is not quite complete yet, but every effort has been made to push the work forward in the hope that when the system is opened for passenger traffic the section will be quite ready to meet what is required of it. Here again the island platform system is found; the buildings are disposed similarly to those north of Loughborough; and the arrangements for goods and mineral traffic and cattle are exactly on all fours with those in other places. The platform of the station measures the regulation 400 feet, and the goods warehouse, situated to the right as the observer faces London, is 40 yards long. There is a water supply for locomotives at either end of the station, immediately to the south of which Mr. Murgatroyd, the new district engineer, resides in a fine old house standing in grounds part of which the company had to take for purposes connected with the construction of the track.

On the whole section from Nottingham to Loughborough the goods sidings, signalling apparatus, and general accessories are practically ready for working, there yet remaining the inevitable final touches to be added at the last moment. For the information contained in this article we are indebted to the kindness and courtesy of Mr. L. G. Felkin, who conducted our representative over the section.

DIVERSION OF THE RIVER SOAR NEAR LOUGHBOROUGH

FROM LOUGHBOROUGH TO LEICESTER

After leaving Loughborough the line runs under Beeches-lane, which is bridged by girders and jack arches, and connects the Loughborough-road. Tuckers' sidings are passed, on the left, with the brickfield which they are intended to serve. Another bridge of plate girders and bricks on an exceedingly sharp skew joins the main road between Leicester and Loughborough, underneath which the railway passes immediately afterwards. Just before this however, are seen the Loughborough Nursery Gardens through the centre of which the Great Central cuts direct.

It may here be mentioned that for practically the whole of the way between Loughborough and Leicester a good view is obtained of the Charnwood Hills, and the picturesque country in the vicinity of Woodhouse Eaves, a district which is highly favoured for its scenery. After Loughborough the first stop is made at the Quorndon and Woodhouse Eaves Station, which, like all the stations on this system, is arranged upon the island plan. The line goes through upon each side and there is a small yard for local traffic, while some 200 yards further along is situated the horse and cattle dock.

Quorn village lies to the left, and so, too, a little further on does Mount Sorrel, famous for its quarries and for the granite-like stones which constitute such serviceable "ballast" for railway purposes. The entire line, all along the section, is laid with these "Mountsorrels," and a walk over the permanent way from Loughborough to the county town is by no means entirely attended with comfort. But patrons of the Great Central will not, of course, be concerned with this as they are whisked along in the company's luxurious corridor cars. For them the journey will be one of supreme ease.

Hereabouts the landscape is of an open and pleasant character. The line runs through the borders of a famous hunting country, with breezy uplands, smiling pastures, and well-wooded plantations stretching away upon either hand. The triumphs and the tribulations of the hunting field are born in upon the imagination by the impenetrable "bullfinches," the stiff "oxers," and the grimly uncompromising "post and rails" which meet the eye everywhere.

From thoughts of the chase the mind turns to a more prosaic, albeit far more practical and utilitarian, subject - Leicester and its water supply. The traveller is now abreast of Swithland Reservoir, which furnishes Leicester people with some of their water. The Swithland Reservoir was constructed by the Leicester Corporation a short time ago, subsequent to the threatened water famine which at one period caused such anxiety. The filter beds and pumping station first attract attention, and a few hundred yards further down the full extent of this splendid sheet of water is unfolded to the eye. It would be difficult, taking any point in the line, to mention any more charming example of sylvan scenery than that which is to be seen at Swithland.

Crossing the reservoir, the line cuts through the corner of a pretty little spot called Brazil Wood, which runs down to the waterside, and a prominent object is the huge submerged dam which bisects the reservoir towards the southern end. One turns reluctantly from Swithland and its delightful surroundings to the hard facts concerned with the work of the engineer at this particular point. The line crosses the reservoir on two short viaducts, of which the first consists of five arches, each of 30 feet span. The second viaduct contains nine arches of 30 feet span, and one girder opening on the skew, also 30 feet span. The slopes of the banks, where they enter the reservoir, are pitched with stone, in order to prevent the water from washing away the banking.

A little distance ahead the Swithland road has to be crossed by means of a girder bridge on brick abutments, and there are here a few coal sidings. Sidings have also been built at Swithland, for the purpose of affording additional facilities to the Mount Sorrel quarries, and sufficient space has also been left between the main lines here to allow of the erection of a passenger station, if at any future time such increased accommodation should be thought necessary. Round a gentle curve the train runs into Rothley Station. The latter is entered by the intending passenger by means of steps leading from the two-arch bridge by which the Rothley-road crosses the line.

Leaving Rothley Station behind, we pass out on to a heavy bank, 40ft. in height, from the foot of which the country gradually rises upon each side. To the east is an exceptionally interesting landmark in Rothley Temple, the birthplace of Lord Macaulay, and to the west is situated the quaint little old-world village of Thurcaston. For the next mile and a half the journey cannot by any stretch of imagination be regarded as interesting, except from the engineering point of view. The passenger might well be excused for having recourse to his papers and periodicals. For 40ft. above the carriages tower the blank staring walls of one of the biggest cuttings to be met with upon the extension. This constituted a serious obstacle to the progress of the work, but Mr. Lovatt's army of workmen, aided by that embodiment of resistless and relentless power, the steam navvy, soon cut their way through the hillside, emerging at a point just north of Birstall and Belgrave.

In this connection may be related a legend which the country folk round about are fond of repeating. It is really nothing more than a play upon names with the connecting thread of a ridiculous story, but it is a bit of Leicestershire folk lore, and so it may be given for what it is worth. Many hundreds of years ago, so the legend goes, there lived in the district a family of giants, named Bell. They were keen sportsmen, mighty hunters, and great riders, and the head of the family is alleged one day to have mounted his sorrel steed at Mount Sorrel, and taken one huge leap to Wanlip. Upon arriving there he pricked spurs again and, leaping into air once more, alighted at Birstall, where he burst all (sic) his girths. Nothing daunted, however, the doughty Bell urged his horse to a last effort, and landed at Belgrave, where both animal and rider fell dead. They were buried here, hence the name, Bell's grave, or Belgrave. So much for the Leicestershire legend.

A big tunnel bridge pierces the bank a short distance beyond Birstall Station, in order to allow the Leicester to Thurcaston-road to pass through. Mowmacre Hill stands out prominently to the west, and the houses of

Belgrave are clearly in view ahead. We are rapidly nearing Leicester. On the left side of the line may be discerned the ruins of Leicester abbey, where Cardinal Wolsey died, and on the east is Beaumont Leys, where is situated the Leicester sewage farm. Beaumont Leys-road being crossed by a 40ft. arch. Abbey-lane coal sidings, which are designed to serve Belgrave and the northern part of the town, having been left in the rear, we arrive, just north of the River Soar, at the tremendous viaduct, which, continuing for a total length of a mile, brings the train at last to Leicester passenger station, which is situated about the middle of the viaduct.

BRAUNSTONE GATE BRIDGE, LEICESTER.
FROM THE GREAT CENTRAL GOODS YARD

THE WORKS AT LEICESTER

At few places along the extension has the construction of the new line necessitated work of a more interesting character than at Leicester. The operations necessitated here have been exactly contradistinctive to those pursued at Nottingham. While in this city the character of the ground has called for extensive tunnelling, boring, and cutting, at Leicester the line runs through on an exceptionally long viaduct, the station occupying a position at a point in the vicinity of the centre of the town. Throughout this section the work has been under the capable superintendence of Mr. Geo. B. Chalcraft, Assoc. M. Inst. C.E., who has been stationed at Leicester as Mr. Parry's representative.

Beyond the construction of the mammoth viaduct, and the placing of the bridges, several of which are of enormous size, no engineering difficulties of very special character have been encountered, although the foundations have given some trouble. The line cuts clean through a thickly populated district, and as the neighbourhood is not one of the best to be met with in Leicester the railway company have probably saved the Corporation the trouble of considering upon some future occasion the question as to what should be done in relation to improving the property. There were a very large number of houses of the poorer class, as well as a number of places of business, including factories and breweries. The company have been compelled to erect 250 cottages in place of the tenements which were destroyed, these being built at Newfound Pool and on the Bow Bridge estate.

Several streets have had, as a matter of course, to be diverted, and one or two new thoroughfares have been established, notably Great Central-street, the handsome roadway in which is situated the entrance to the station, and which extends from St. Nicholas-street to Northgate-street. Great Central-street is 50 feet wide throughout, ample space being requisite for the reception of the heavy traffic which is expected to make use of the thoroughfare when the line is in full working order.

The viaduct commences at Harrison-street, north of the River Soar, which is crossed by a girder bridge, as is also Abbey-gate, which adjoins it. The railway is taken over the river by a two-span girder, and another bridge of a similar character crosses Slater-street. After crossing over the canal the railway comes to Northgate-street bridge, upon the other side of which the line spreads out upon either hand in order to accommodate the station which is of very substantial size. Platforms are about a quarter of a mile in length. The station will, by the way, be described in detail at a later stage of this article, at present it will serve a more useful purpose to deal with the streets, bridges and constructive work which had to be completed before the buildings overhead were concerned.

A little distance along the southern side of the station is Welles-street, which is another new thoroughfare. Bath-lane, another girder bridge over the river Soar, St. Augustine-street, Westbridge-street, Braunstone-gate bridge,

BRIDGE OVER BRAUNSTONE GATE, LEICESTER

and lastly, a girder bridge over the old Soar, which is retained by the Corporation as a flood course. Some idea of the arduous labour for which the placing in position of these ponderous structures called, may be afforded by a few particulars giving the length of several of the principal ones, together with the approximate weights of the metal used in their construction.

The first long span bridge occurs at the northern extremity of the viaduct, and crosses the Soar, the girders being 88 feet long. The Northgate-street bridge is set at an angle so acute that it makes a skew span of 107 feet long, which is more than double the length of the square span. As it bears on the abutment the big girder is 137 feet in length, and the steel in the whole bridge would weigh about 300 tons. All Saints'-road bridge contains about 350 tons of steel work, and the extent of the roadway covered in is over 190 feet. The reason for this tunnel-like covering of the street lies in the fact that the station is approached exactly at this point, and the line, as previously indicated, commences here to spread out.

Prior to being taken in hand by the contractors All Saints'-street was quite a narrow thoroughfare. It has now been both widened and lowered, the latter proceeding being necessary in order to accommodate the heavy vehicular traffic which passes underneath. Owing to the width of the bridge, the conditions below are somewhat tunnel-like, and the company have lined the street on each side with glazed bricks, with the object of increasing the light. This purpose has been admirably effected.

Another immense structure is the skew bridge traversing Braunstone-gate, which carries the line over the Soar and the old flood course. One of the girders is 175 and the other 136 feet long, and the bridge contains 400 tons weight of steel. Owing to the nature of the ground upon which the station stands the work of laying the foundation firmly constituted an exceptionally formidable feature of the operations at Leicester, and it is a curious fact that, by far the greatest portion of the work here is buried out of sight. The foundations of the platforms, for instance, are 30ft. below the top of the platform. The chief reason for this is forthcoming in the circumstances that a layer of something like 12ft. of loose black soil was first encountered.

The station stands actually on the site of the original Roman city, and it is thought probable that this soil has been gradually accumulating ever since the time of the Roman occupation. Leicester, as is well known, was once a Roman stronghold, and over an area extending from the Great Central goods yard on the south to Birstall on the north Roman pottery, implements, weapons, and other evidence of this, including even human remains, have been found. But the most interesting relic of all was not left for the railway contractor to discover.

Many years ago, to be exact, in 1832, while certain excavations were being proceeded with upon the site of the Old Jewry Wall, the workmen suddenly came upon a portion of a Roman pavement in a remarkably fine state of preservation. With the laudable object of still further preserving to future generations this artistic survival of ancient methods, the Corporation built a

LEICESTER PASSENGER STATION

house above the pavement and appointed a caretaker, whose successors have, throughout the years which have elapsed since then, continued to exhibit their charge to wondering spectators. But, as it happened, the Great Central extension ran exactly over the spot, and the company have been compelled to build a large, light and airy chamber over the pavement, which is entrusted to the care of a neighbourhood shopkeeper, and remains the property of the Corporation. And so it falls out that the handiwork of the craftsmen of bygone days is, by the strangest of chances, retained underneath a modern railway station.

The race to the Metropolis will be conducted over the ground where once the Roman legions marched, but the cunningly-contrived mosaic floor, with its quaint designs, its scrolls, its traceries and squares, as it winds in and out in irregular outline, now faint, now boldly distinct, in the brick and mortar setting provided for it years ago by a thoughtful Corporation, will, undisturbed by the rude hand of the contractor, continue this third and strangest phase of its existence, attracting as before, the archaeologically inclined, the curious, and the studious.

Turn we once again to the consideration of matters more practical. The station, with its arrangements and equipments, now claims attention. It is laid out upon the island principle. That is to say, when once the passengers have gained access to the platform by means of the subways leading from the street they will be able to reach any train without being compelled to cross the line. The main lines extend along each side of the platform, while at both ends of the station deep bays have been let in for the purposes of the local traffic, which, it is anticipated, will be very heavy. The blind end of each bay is fitted with two sets of hydraulic buffer stoppers, constructed upon the latest principle. These buffers project four of five feet from the stops, and it is considered that in the event of any unforeseen contingency arising they will absorb the force of the blow, precluding the possibility of the engine or train passing beyond their limits.

There are in the station six sets of through rails, in addition to a number of sidings. Arrangements for watering the engines have been made at both ends of the station, and a turn-table for reversing the locomotives is established on the south-east side, adjacent to the site selected for the erection of the company's own district engineer's office. Close to the turn-table, and approached from Great Central-street, is the horse and carriage dock. The dispersion of the sewage has been considered with close attention to elaborate detail, and upon this score the arrangements are characterised by the utmost completeness.

The sewers are laid in a subway, which runs all round the blocks of buildings, the pipes for the two north blocks being connected upon the east side with the street, those for the south block being connected on the west to the street sewer. As the sewer subways are upon a higher level than the street, tumbling bays are instituted close to the connecting point. The storm water is conveyed from the roof gullies down the supporting pillars, and the

LEICESTER GOODS YARD, SHOWING UPPERTON VIADUCT

subways throughout their whole extent are sufficiently lofty to admit of a minute survey being made of the sewage system.

The south block of station buildings contains the stationmaster's and clerks' offices, inspectors' and telegraph office, lavatories, and general waiting-rooms. The latter are both light and airy, skylights being introduced in addition to the windows. Floors, doors, and window frames are of pitch-pine. A large portion of the plaster used in the rooms is of the fibrous kind, which is sent completely fashioned, and ready for immediate application. By this means a vast amount of time and labour is saved.

Signal boxes are established at each end of the station, and another is fixed in the centre of the platform, the sides being carried out to enable the signalman to sight both up and down main lines. The centre block of buildings contains the refreshment department, the dining-room being in the middle, and the first and third-class refreshment-rooms at either end. Downstairs are the kitchens, larders, and wine and beer cellars, and all the provisions and supplies are to be brought direct by a sub-way leading from Great Central-street. In the north block are more waiting-rooms, including first and third-class apartments for the use of lady passengers.

It will be observed that while the station buildings at Nottingham are of glazed bricks, those at the Leicester station have the ordinary reds and terracottas. The reason for this distinction is contained in the fact that while the Nottingham station lies in a cutting that at Leicester is situated at the top of a viaduct. The glazed bricks are requisitioned at the former place for the purposes of improving the light.

Booking offices, left-luggage stores, cloak-rooms, &c., are all situated below, close to the main entrance in Great Central-street, and are reached from the platforms by steps leading to the sub-way. The entrance for cabs, parcel vans, &c., is in Great Central-street, and a number of cabs are to stand in the large covered yard, which is roofed with glass. For the convenience of passengers arriving on foot from the west side, another subway connected with the main passage, leads from the street at that point. On the level are, therefore, three subways, of which that in the middle is intended solely to convey luggage to the huge lift, those at the side being for the use of the passengers. Adequate light in the subways is ensured by the adoption of the Heywood patent and glazed bricks.

The frontage to the Great Central Station has a very handsome appearance. The brickwork is very admirable in design, and the fine clock tower over the principal gateway gives a finishing touch to what is quite an imposing entrance.

In the goods yard the arrangements are almost precisely similar to those which prevail at Nottingham. Access to the goods yard is obtained from Western-boulevard. The offices are close to the new Newarke Bridge, which has been recently built by the Corporation, and about a third of the way down, on the east side, stands a large hydraulic and electrical building. The goods yard at the south end is crossed by a long viaduct leading from Walnut-street

Bridge to the Narborough-road. Here are also the cattle pens and loading docks, and about the north middle are the goods warehouses and a large number of coal and general sidings. A large space has been left in order that the accommodation may, if necessary, be increased.

The west side of the yard is occupied by the carriage shed and oil gas works, the waggon repairing shop being a little distance away to the south. Still further towards the southern portion of the yard, and just before coming to the Midland Railway bridge from Leicester to Burton, is the locomotive shed, which will accommodate 20 engines, the equipment being upon the usual lines. In the goods yard, as in relation to other portions of the work at Leicester, the chief difficulty which had to be faced lay in the foundations which, owing to the soft nature of the soil, go down 18 or 20 feet. No doubt the bed of the river has shifted some time or another, and the excavators came upon the silt.

An interesting fact which may, in concluding this article, be mentioned, is the circumstance that immediately to the west of the passenger station lies the Midland Leicester to Swannington line, one of the oldest railways in England.

LEICESTER TO RUGBY

The section connecting Leicester with Rugby, viewed from a picturesque point standpoint, can hardly be said to present any particularly interesting features, although, regarded in the light of railway enterprise, it is admittedly one of the best lengths on the whole route, and, in as much as the gradient between the two towns rarely exceeds 1 in 176, the rate of travelling can be considerably accelerated as occasion demands.

Commencing at Aylestone, which forms a part of the municipal borough of Leicester, the line cuts through 16 miles of purely agricultural and rich pasture land, the section undertaken by Messrs. Topham, Jones, and Railton, the contractors, terminating at the Oxford Canal, about a mile north of the station at Rugby. It is a double railroad throughout, and the signalling has been executed in accordance with modern requirements by the Railway Signal Company, Liverpool.

Immediately on leaving Aylestone the line is carried over the Northampton Union Canal on a bridge of the plate girder type, with lattice parapets, the span being about 60 feet in width, and in close proximity to the canal is noticeable a very antiquated Roman bridge, concerning which the residents in that district relate some interesting historical reminiscences. South of the canal the line crosses the valley of the River Sence on the Whetstone viaduct, a brick structure having 13 openings of 30 feet with semi-circular arches, the total length of the viaduct is 455 feet. The engineer deemed it expedient to make some slight diversions for the River Sence, and significant alterations were effected.

South of the Whetstone viaduct the line crosses the London and North-Western system (Leicester and Nuneaton branch), being carried over by a plate girder bridge, with a span of 66ft., in the construction of which about 150 tons of steel were used. Provision has been made to allow for the widening of the North-Western Railway in view of any such future necessity arising.

Following a pretty district course, the line runs on to a very long embankment, containing nearly a million cubic yards of earthwork, and representing nearly two years' work. It reaches about 42ft. at its highest point, and situated upon it is Whetstone Station, approached from the main road by a bridge. The station is constructed on the principle generally adopted by the company, the buildings being of red brick and including ladies' and gentlemen's waiting-rooms respectively, booking office, accommodation for porters, and the ordinary conveniences. Island platforms have been built, and notwithstanding the fact that only two roads are completed, there is available space for their extension when necessary, and for the erection of a goods warehouse as the traffic increases.

Separated from the station itself, a comfortable-looking detached residence has been built for the stationmaster overlooking the premises, and a goods office and siding have also been provided, the latter embodying a granite tipping dock for the convenience of certain companies at Croft and

THREE ARCH SKEW BRIDGE ON THE LEICESTER TO RUGBY SECTION

Stoney Stanton, two pleasant little villages a mile and a half from Whetstone, where the majority of the inhabitants are employed in a large syenite rock quarry worked by steam power. The manufacture of bricks and concrete is also extensively prosecuted there.

From the embankment an excellent and comprehensive view of the surrounding country is obtainable, the little church of St. Peter's at Whetstone, a handsome early English structure, erected, according to an inscription on the north buttress, in 1335, standing out prominently and in happy contrast to innumerable little red houses heaped together right in the centre of the parish.

Just south of Whetstone, a three arch tunnel bridge is erected. This carries the Whetstone brook in the centre opening, and two additional flood openings have also been provided, to avert the possibility of any danger. A long skew arch bridge with about 15 feet of embankment on the top crosses the Narborough-road, and with the exception of about five public road bridges of the plate girder type, with lattice parapets, the work was tolerably easy until the line crosses the Midland Railway (Leicester to Rugby branch) north of the Leicester turnpike road. Here it runs into a cutting nearly two miles long, over which the Leicester turnpike road is carried by a three arch skew bridge at an angle of 40 deg., the span being about 40 feet on the square.

Engineering skill removed several technical difficulties which confronted the contractors, and although in the cutting itself a considerable quantity of water was found, it was very carefully drained, trenches being dug out and filled with granite. There was a good deal of running sand in the cutting, and in certain places the slopes had to be pitched with granite. About 300,000 cubic yards of soil had to be excavated, most of this conveyed north to form part of the Whetstone and Cosby embankment. We reproduce the bridge and cutting from a photograph view taken specially for the purpose.

At the end of the cutting the line continues over a small embankment crossing two public roads en route and pursuing an almost straight course, runs into Ashby Magna Station. It is approached from the road by a stepway, and possesses, in addition to passenger' accommodation, a siding for coal and general goods. The station is rather pleasantly situated between Ashby Magna and Dunton Bassett. The last-named is claimed to be an ancient village, the houses in some instances bearing old dates, and displaying other indications of antiquity.

On leaving the station the road bends slightly to the right, and runs into a deep cutting, in the middle of which a short tunnel, 94 yards in length, has been cut through blue clay, and bands of gravel and pockets of sand. The section of the tunnel is egg-shaped, differing from those at Nottingham, and faced with brindle bricks and stone. In its construction the greatest care had to be exercised in drawing the timber, and the sides were packed out with straw, these precautionary measures being adopted against the danger apprehended from the fineness of the sand. A public road is carried over the tunnel, the extreme width of the latter being 27 feet, and its height 26 feet from the metals to the crown.

LUTTERWORTH STATION

At Cotes de Val, an aristocratic name for a hamlet of one farm of 313 acres, not far from Gilmorton, the line is continued over a short valley by an embankment 32ft. high and runs into a small cutting, the public road for Gilmorton to Ashby being crossed by a three-arch brick bridge built on the square, the centre span measuring 26 feet, and the two outer ones 20 feet each. Sweeping on through a stretch of magnificent hunting country Lutterworth Station furnishes the next point of interest.

In proportion to the importance of the town, the station buildings are constructed perhaps upon a trifle more elaborate scale, possessing an extensive goods yard and an exceedingly attractive entrance. Lutterworth itself is a nice old-fashioned town, pleasantly situated on the banks of the River Swift, a feeder of the Avon, and closely borders on the counties of Northamptonshire and Warwickshire respectively. It is rich in historic associations, and boasts of a handsome church of stone in the early decorated style, containing numerous carefully preserved indications of antiquity, which are intensely interesting.

Over the chancel arch is a singular fresco representing the "general resurrection" brought to light during the restoration, and over the north door are three life-sized figures, said to represent Richard II., Anne (his wife), and John of Gaunt, Duke of Lancaster, the friend and patron of John Wickliffe, the great reformer, who was rector of Lutterworth from 1374 until 1384, and whose portrait is preserved in the church together with the remnant of a cope, popularly supposed to have been his. He died on the last day of the year 1384, and was buried in the village, but in1428, in pursuance of a decree of the Council of Constance in 1415, his remains were exhumed, burnt, and the ashes cast into the River Swift.

The town is the seat of no particular manufacture, its trade principally consisting in supplying the agricultural interest of the neighbourhood.

Directly after leaving Lutterworth the line passes over the River Swift by means of a tunnel bridge, with a 45ft. span and 10ft. of embankment on the top. The bridge is built of brick, the river running through a concrete carrier down the centre. The main road from Lutterworth to Market Harborough is crossed by a 40ft. span brick bridge, and a short distance further south, beyond a small cutting, a three-arch bridge, constructed on the skew, carries another highway. Following this is a little embankment, and then the line enters a cutting comparatively shallow, but nearly two miles in extent. There were nearly 300,000 yards of excavation rendered necessary, but the difficulties encountered were remarkably few, the discovery of a quantity of water being the only thing to contend with, and this was easily overcome by an efficient system of drainage.

Just north of Watling-street, which runs under a brick arch bridge, with a span of 40ft., on the square, a very considerable quantity of material has been tipped with a view at some future period of providing a station for Showell and Newton. Continuing a practically straight course through vast stretches of undulating land, the line runs into what is known as Newton Cutting, adjoining which is a ballast pit to be used for the repair and maintenance of the permanent way. A good deal has already been excavated for embankments along the road. Close to the pit a public road crosses the cutting at a point where it is estimated to be 40 feet deep, and for the purposes of carrying it a five arch bridge had to be erected very much on the skew at an angle of 56 degrees. It is built entirely of brick, and its total length is 222ft., there being five spans including one of 30ft. and two each of 26ft. and 28ft. respectively on the square.

The cutting runs out on to a short embankment, and into another shallow cutting over the river Avon, the latter being crossed by a 45ft. span tunnel bridge faced with brindle bricks, with about 10ft. of embankment on top, very similar to that over the Swift. Four chains beyond this where the bank is about 45ft. high and close to the Oxford Canal the section undertaken by Messrs. Topham, Jones, and Railton terminates. Throughout the whole 16 miles, singularly enough, not an inch of rock had to be removed, and practically no remains whatever were found in excavating.

RUGBY TO QUAINTON ROAD

The serious differences which have arisen between the directorates and management of the Great Central and the Metropolitan Railway Companies are matters of common knowledge, and the public have also been acquainted with the fact that the Great Central Company have entered into, and completed, negotiations with the Great Western Company with the object of providing an alternative route to the Metropolis. Should Parliamentary sanction for the new scheme be obtained the original plans will necessarily be completely altered, and instead of travelling some 40 odd miles from Quainton-road, on Metropolitan metals, the Great Central trains will run over only three, Marylebone being reached by means of the Great Western system, through Grendon Underwood, Princes Risborough, High Wycombe, and Neasden. This involves no little additional expense, and a somewhat lengthened journey, but the gradients are better, and the Great Central regard the project with every favour.

For the present, however, the route to London for all practical purposes is that which carries the company from Rugby, through Willoughby, Charwelton, Woodford, and Hinton, Culworth, Helmdon, Brackley, Finmere, and Calvert, to Quainton-road, and thence over 42 miles of Metropolitan Railway to Finchley-road. From this point the Great Central have laid down two miles of independent lines to their terminal station, Marylebone. Along the whole length of this, the Southern and Metropolitan section of the extension, the chief engineers were Sir Douglas Fox, the company's consulting engineer, aided by his brother, Mr. Francis Fox, and as on other portions of the line the work has been characterised by most careful attention to the minutest detail.

The heavy rains of January, and the early part of last month made a severe strain upon the embankments, but they have stood the test remarkably well, and the goods traffic which has been in progress since July has served materially to aid in their consolidation. Here and there occasional slips have occurred, but the southern section has been splendidly constructed, and, with the length from Annesley to Rugby, completes an undertaking which from the engineering point of view has been accomplished with striking success.

Heavy earth works may be said to constitute the chief feature of the section, but tunnelling operations near the terminal station, and the vast area at Marylebone for the accommodation of traffic of all kinds, involved an unusual expenditure of labour and capital, and midway between Rugby and Woodford - where extensive engine and carriage sheds are located - there is a tunnel of 3,000 yards, which holds the record for length on the whole extension. The section includes five viaducts, 46 bridges, 32 culverts, 12 cuttings, and 13 embankments, in addition to the Gatesby tunnel.

Just to the north of the London and North-Western Company's main line at Rugby, the first contract on the southern section commences, and the construction of the new line herefrom to Woodford, was entrusted to Messrs.

CROSSING THE L. AND N.-W., AT RUGBY, LOOKING NORTH

T. Oliver and Sons, of Rugby. Almost at the beginning of their section the contractors were called upon to erect a viaduct upwards of 300 yards long, on a slight curve, carrying the Great Central over the Oxford Canal and the London and North-Western system, the girder bridge above the latter being of huge proportions. Stringent regulations were enforced as to the non-interference with the traffic below during the progress of the work, but the difficulties, though great, were happily surmounted.

Hilmorton-road crosses the line at the extreme end of the viaduct, and it is from this thoroughfare that the Rugby Station is reached, by means of a covered staircase. Though far from comparing in magnitude with the imposing structure on the neighbouring system, the station at Rugby is, in common with others of the new type, adopted by the Great Central Railway, an exceedingly convenient and pretty building, admirably equipped.

Between Rugby and Willoughby and Braunston, the next stopping place, there is a fine cutting two miles long, from which no fewer than a million and a quarter cubic yards were excavated, and from the cutting the lines run out on to a twelve-arch viaduct in the Willoughby parish. At Staverton-road, a short distance to the south of Willoughby, there is another viaduct of eleven arches, and it was at this point that a serious landslip, caused by the heavy rains, occurred early in February. The work of repairing the damage occupied many days, and the goods trains were worked on single line during its progress.

Gatesby tunnel, which runs under a range of hills for 3,000 yards, has to be traversed ere Charwelton is reached. Rocky formations were frequently met with during boring operations, and unlike the tunnels at Nottingham, where the sandstone rock served as supports to the arch, the walls throughout had to be thickly lined with brindle bricks. The work was of a very heavy character, and its completion stands as an excellent example of the skill and ingenuity alike of the engineers and contractors.

Woodford and Hinton, the next station to Charwelton, claims special attention, in that it forms the seat of administrative operations on a large scale. Apart from the space for the main lines the company here purchased 25 acres of land for the erection of engine and carriage repairing sheds, and the construction of extensive sidings. The route at this point lay across a valley of pasture land, and the whole of the acreage had to be "tipped" with material from the cuttings so as to bring the works on a level with the main line. Woodford has until recently been but a sleepy village, but the arrival of the railway company has changed the order, and some 140 new houses have been built, or are in course of erection, to accommodate the small army of workmen who will be located there.

The engine shed has been built to hold 40 engines, and it is of the most approved pattern, with six sets of rails. Commodious offices for the locomotive foremen and clerks are provided, together with a capital mess room for the workmen, stores, smithy, lathe shop, with every possible appurtenance, even to an overhead traveller to carry the wheels from the shed to the lathe. A 30 horse power semi-vertical engine, from Messrs. Ruston Proctor, and Company of Lincoln, supplies the motive power, and on either side of the shed there is a huge hoist for lifting damaged engines whenever necessity arises. A 15 ton steam crane, and vans fitted with all the materials for use of the break-down gang, are also located in the engine-shed, and just outside there is another hoist for use in fine weather, and in the case of urgently needed repairs.

Adjoining the engine-shed the contractors have erected an extensive sheet repairing shop, next to which is situated the carriage repairing shed, a long building with three sets of rails. A sand-drying furnace, coal stage, turn-table, and water tower, with a capacity for 100,000 gallons have been erected on the east side of the goods yard, and nearer to the station are the buildings which accommodate the electric lighting plant, for the illumination of all the workshops and sidings. In close proximity are the offices for the traffic inspector and the guards, and a large plot of land has been reserved for the coal stack. In view of possible contingencies the company intend to store about 10,000 tons of coal at Woodford.

The sidings contain seven sets of rails, apart from the two goods, and the two main lines which run straight through, and the points throughout the whole yard are controlled from four signal cabins, that on the main line to the south of the station having 76 levers.

Just below Woodford and Hinton station Messrs. Oliver and Sons had to construct a loop line from the Great Central Railway to form a junction at Byfield station with the East to West Railway. This allows of an interchange of traffic with the London and North-Western and Midland Railways, by giving access to Towcester and Stratford-on-Avon. The contractors for the section from Woodford South Junction to Quainton-road, Messrs. Walter Scott and Co., of Newcastle, and Westminster, undertook the connection with the same loop line from the southern end, and midway between the two junctions the responsibilities of Messrs. Oliver and Sons ceased.

Messrs. Walter Scott and Co. found themselves confronted throughout practically the whole length of their section - 25½ miles - with earthworks of the heaviest possible character, and the stretch of line from Woodford, almost to the junction with the Metropolitan railway at Quainton-road is one succession of extremely deep cuttings, and high embankments with two short and substantial viaducts.

Close to Eydon village, which lies equi-distant between Woodford and Culworth, occurs the commencement of the branch railway, which is to carry the Great Central on to the Great Western system at Banbury. The branch, eight-and-a-half miles in length, is at present in course of construction, and will, in all probability, be completed this year. Its chief feature is a long cutting from which nearly 1,000,000 cubic yards of earth have been removed. The junction with the Great Western Railway at Banbury and further south at Grendon Underwood are likely to be extremely advantageous to the Great Central Railway.

From Culworth station passengers will be able to obtain a fine view of the village of Sulgrave, historically interesting by reason of the fact that it was the birthplace and residence of George Washington's forefathers. South of Culworth the railway passes through the Barrow cutting, and reaches the highest point on the run from Rugby to the Metropolis. A viaduct of nine arches crosses the Northampton and Banbury junction railway at Helmdon, and on the way to Brackley a peep can be secured of a very quaint little church at Radstone.

Brackley has been provided with a commodious station, and goods warehouse, and within a hundred yards or so of the station there is a fine viaduct of 20 arches spanning the valley of the Ouse at a height of 70 feet. Originally it was intended that the viaduct should consist of 22 arches, but an unforeseen slip in the embankment at the southern end compelled the contractors to erect two massive girder spans.

Though boasting a population according to the census for 1891, of but 2,591 souls, Brackley possesses a charter of incorporation, and until the passing of the Reform Bill in 1832, returned two members of Parliament. At the present time it forms a convenient centre for a magnificent hunting country which provides sport for the Grafton, Bletchley, and Bicester hunts.

South of Brackley viaduct there is a girder bridge which carries the Great Central over the London and North-Western Company's lines from Bletchley to Banbury, and from this point the extension passes through Finmere and Calvert stations to Quainton-road the work over this distance having been of an exceedingly light character. Throughout their entire section Messrs. Walter Scott and Co. removed some three and a half million cubic yards of earth, and erected between 90,000 and 100,000 cubic yards of brickwork, faced throughout with blue and brindled bricks. The line from Woodford to Quainton-road is ballasted with slag, obtained from the furnaces at Wellingborough and Kettering.

BRACKLEY VIADUCT

THE NEW TERMINAL STATION

The agreement with the Metropolitan Railway Company gives the Great Central running powers from Quainton-road to Finchley-road, but there are no stations en route at which the latter are to be allowed to take up or set down passengers, and they will, for the present at any rate, be compelled to travel 42 miles under restricted conditions, until they arrive at their own independent lines again at Finchley-road. Two miles from that point they reach their new terminal station at Marylebone, and its adjacent goods-yard, of vast proportions.

The contract for the London end was let to Messrs. Joseph T. Firbank and Son, of London, and some idea of the magnitude of their task may be gathered from the fact that, in spite of unremitting energy, the work, at least in regard to goods traffic, is not yet quite completed.

From Finchley-road to St. John's Wood the new line traverses a succession of tunnels and covered ways, alongside the Metropolitan Company's metals, and finally emerges into the terminal station-yard from a "cut and cover," 212 yards long, under Lord's Cricket Ground. Preparations have also been made for the construction of a second tunnel, and an additional pair of rails from Finchley-road.

In addition to the two main lines, there are five sets of sidings under the cricket ground and St. John's Wood-road, and these seven lines are increased to eleven in number ere the bridge over the Regent's Canal is reached. This extreme width involved the construction of a very large bridge over the canal, and its design was as elaborate as its erection was difficult. No fewer than 13 of the girders were built upon the skew, and there are 950 tons of steel work in the bridge altogether.

At the back of the St. John's Wood station, on the Metropolitan Railway, there is a 94-lever signal cabin, controlling the entrance to the goods-yard, the lay-bye sheds, and the coal depot, which lie to the west of the passenger lines. From the Regent's Canal the latter fall on a gradient of 1 in 100 to the Marylebone station. In their course they are crossed by a very fine steel girder bridge of six spans, which carries the Rossmore-road. This is an entirely new thoroughfare, one of several made by the company to replace the streets and roads which were absorbed in the preparation of the area for the purposes of the railway, and provides direct communication with the goods yard, in addition to affording a more convenient approach by means of a sloping road to the terminal station for vehicular traffic.

It is highly probable that there will be a station on the Baker-street and Waterloo railway now in course of construction, close to Rossmore-road, and that it will communicate with the Great Central terminus by a subway.

By the side of the main lines the contractors have erected fish and milk platforms, and horse-loading docks, with a separate entrance from Hill-street, a small thoroughfare communicating with Rossmore-road, and still further to the east are situated a carriage shed 480 feet long, by 42 feet wide, oil gas works, on Pope's system, and a turntable.

Marylebone Station itself is a spacious structure, substantially built, brightly decorated, and splendidly lighted. The erection of the handsome and imposing Hotel Great Central, fronting the Marylebone-road, obviated the necessity of investing the facade of the station proper with any elaborate architectural ornamentations, but the frontage, which is 340 feet long, nevertheless looks remarkably well.

It is built of red Leicestershire bricks with terra-cotta dressings, and is reached from Marylebone-road by a broad approach on the east of the new hotel known as Great Central-street. Save for the erection of an awning between the rear of the hotel and the station, and the finishing touches to the roof and the parcels offices, the station is completed. It is a three-storey building, and has upon the first floor a succession of admirable administrative offices, together with an extensive Board room. The booking-hall is a commodious apartment, excellently arranged and tastefully decorated, lined with terra-cotta and glazed bricks, and the refreshment and waiting-rooms possess like characteristics.

Between the station buildings and the platforms there is a promenade or circulating space, 310 ft. long by 100ft. wide, which will serve to relieve the crush of pedestrian traffic on the platforms. A subway connects the refreshment rooms with the hotel. The station embraces at present two main departure and two main arrival platforms, but ample provision is made for an extension to double the present size on the west side, the property in Blandford-square having been acquired for the purpose.

Light and ventilation have been carefully considered in the erection of the station, and glass is utilised for the whole of the promenade roof and 77 per cent. of the platform roof. The latter is in the form of three clerestorys with two spans of a little more than 50ft., and one of rather more than 40ft. The roofs rest upon columns and girders, and cover in all five sets of rails.

The platforms are 25ft. wide in each case, and the cab rank has a uniform width of 30ft. All the vehicles which await the arrival of trains from the North will be compelled to approach the cab rank from Rossmore-road and leave by Great Central-street, a system which is intended to obviate congestion of traffic as far as possible.

Each of the platforms is 900ft. in length, and 400ft. of the total distance is roofed in. The signal-box controlling the station is situated on one of the main departure platforms, and there is another cabin, with 100 levers, to the north of Rossmore-road bridge. The parcels offices and the accommodation for collection and delivery vans are located at the western end of the promenade. Electric arc and Sonsegrayson gas lamps are to be utilised for lighting the whole of the station.

The goods yard lies to the west of the short stretch from the station to Regent's Canal bridge, and being upon a higher level is divided from the main lines by a huge retaining wall. The work of preparing the area for the metropolitan terminus involved the demolition of no fewer than 1,045 houses, and the breaking up of numerous streets, and in the earliest stages the contractors encountered interminable difficulties in dealing with the gas, water, and sewer mains. A visit to the goods yard now affords no idea of the vastness of the undertaking and its commencement, but it provides a striking instance of the mastery which engineering skill has obtained over seemingly insuperable obstacles.

Starting from the northern end of the yard the contractors, in addition to constructing the Regent's Canal bridge, were required to widen the canal by 70ft., and on the south side to form an extensive lay-bye, with a steep retaining wall, faced with Warwickshire brindled bricks. The widening of the canal enables the barges to anchor close to the lay-bye shed, and interchange traffic with the railway company, without interfering with the direct passage of other boats. The lay-bye shed, which is 530ft. long, by 90ft. wide, is covered by what is technically known, as an umbrella roof, and it is equipped with three lines of rails, and a 25 ton travelling hydraulic crane.

In close proximity there is a small engine shed, and just to the south occur the metals for the coal depot, which traverse a falling gradient from the canal bridge, and run into extensive sidings 300 yards long, and about 80 wide, at Grove-road. This portion of the terminus has been in full swing now for some months, and already the company are finding the strain of traffic somewhat too heavy for the space at their disposal. Further extension, indeed, is imperative.

A commodious electric and hydraulic power house, completely fitted with the most modern machinery, abuts upon extensive sidings for working goods into the town carts, a system which is facilitated by the provision of a travelling electric crane, spanning two lines of rails, and capable of lifting 25 tons, and of several smaller cranes. Goods offices on a scale of unusual magnitude have been erected at the western extremity of Rossmore-road, and it is at this point that the main entrance to the goods-yard is situated, within easy distance of the huge warehouse, a five-storey building, with a total floor space of more than eleven acres.

On the main approach there are two machines for weighing carts in and out of the yard, and there is a sloping road from the entrance which leads down to the basement of the warehouse, at its southern end. Hydraulic lifts are to be utilised to lower waggons to the basement at the other end, whenever occasion demands. Upwards of 6,000 tons of steel have been utilised in the erection of the warehouse, all the girders in the basement and on the ground and first floor being of that material. Every conceivable device to facilitate the task of dealing with the goods traffic has been provided, and, in addition to its gigantic size, the warehouse is admirably planned. Innumerable cranes, traversers, and capstans are already in position, and the building is all but complete internally.

Externally the rails to the warehouse are worked on a series of 18 turntables, and there are six roads into the warehouse itself. On the east side there is an extensive dock for standing goods, which it is intended to roof in, and six elevators have been erected to work the whole height of the warehouse. Nothing is more striking in regard to the planning of the goods yard, and the buildings upon it, than the excellent method which has been observed in every detail, and, notwithstanding its great extent, upwards of 70 acres, the area is remarkably compact.

In enumerating the works which the contractors were called upon to undertake, mention must not be omitted of the construction of several new streets, of stabling, and other conveniences, for the coal merchants in the Grove-road depot, and of the provision of vast stabling near the St. John's Wood-road for Messrs. Thompson and McKay, the company's carting agents.

Hemmed in by many difficulties, the Great Central have nevertheless, in their determination to reach the Metropolis, provided yet another addition to the notable railway undertakings which have so strongly marked the commercial and engineering progress of the Victorian era, and the London terminus stands as a fitting climax of their undaunted enterprise.

Outside the station, and facing the road, a magnificent hotel, hereafter to be known as the Hotel Great Central, has been erected. Architecturally the building, which is in Leicestershire red brick, with terra-cotta dressings, compares favourably with most of the similar establishments in London. It is upon a vast scale, containing upwards of 400 rooms, and a fine courtyard, and will be luxuriously appointed. From every point of view, indeed, it affords a further example of the completeness which has been characteristic of the whole undertaking.

At Neasden, a few miles from Marylebone, the company have provided an administrative yard upon an extensive scale. It contains an engine shed capable of accommodating 30 engines, a large water tank, and a sand-drying house, carriage and waggon repairing shops, and ten sorting sidings. At present 20 acres have been utilised, and there is ample room for further extension.

DESPATCH OF THE SPECIAL TRAIN

THE NEW ROLLING STOCK

It had been arranged in connection with to-day's proceedings to run three special trains to London for the purpose of conveying the guests invited to the opening ceremony and subsequent luncheon at Marylebone Station. One of the number was timed to leave London-road Station, Manchester, at eight o'clock in the morning, the second to depart from Sheffield at 9.03, and the third to start from Nottingham at 10.05. The Manchester train, according to preliminary arrangement, was expected to run through to Rugby without a stop, the second to reach Brackley ere it pulled up, while the third was deputed to take up passengers at Loughborough, Leicester, and Woodford and Hinton.

The timetable was so prepared as to enable all the guests from the provinces to arrive at the terminus to meet Mr. Ritchie, who had consented to perform the opening ceremony, at 1.45 pm.

Having regard to the incompleteness of some of the station buildings, notably those at Nottingham and Leicester, there was little in the nature of local demonstrations, but special preparations to signalise the occasion were taken at the three starting points, and keen interest was noticed in the proceedings, many persons assembling in the neighbourhood of the various stations to watch the passage of the trains.

In the case of each of the specials the latest type of rolling stock was used, and on all hands it excited admiration. The train from Manchester was drawn by engine 268, constructed upon the designs recently completed by Mr. Harry Pollitt, M. Inst., C. E., M. Inst., M. E., the company's locomotive engineer. She is a four-wheeled coupled bogie engine, with tender, has a firebox of the Belpaire type, and piston valves below the cylinders in place of the old-time slide valves. Her driving and trailing wheels are 7ft. in diameter, and those of the bogie 3ft. 6in. The tender is capable of carrying 4,000 gallons of water, and five tons of coal on three pairs of wheels each 4ft. 6in. in diameter. The total length of the engine and tender over the buffers is 54ft., and the weight, in working order is 80 tons.

The train was composed of a composite carriage, third class dining saloon, kitchen car, first class dining saloon, first class corridor coach, third class corridor coach, and guards van, the corridor principle being adopted throughout. The carriages rest upon four-wheeled bogies, and, among other contrivances, are fitted with torpedo ventilation, the automatic vacuum brake, communication between passenger and driver and guard by means of the vacuum brake, and electric communication between passengers and attendants. The dining saloon and kitchen car are lighted by electricity, and the remainder by oil gas with Coligny lamps.

Twenty passengers can dine in the first-class saloons, which are finished in rare woods, upholstered in figured plush, and embellished with works of art, the roofs being richly decorated in gold and colours. Bulkheads are of Spanish mahogany, relieved with carvings, fretwork, and satin wood raised panels, and bordered with Coromandel wood. The ends of the compartments are panelled, moulded, and carved to match, and adorned with proof etchings, whilst the doors and insides with marquetry of most effective designs.

Externally the third-class dining saloon is of like design, internally they are finished in light oak the roofs being covered with lincrusts neatly picked out and decorated. They have seating accommodation for 36 diners, and are provided with clerestory roofs and stained glass lights.

The platforms at the end of each of the dining cars are finished, both outside and inside, with bevel-edged glass doors, and all the side lights are of bevelled edged glass in frames of teak wood. The kitchen car comprises the kitchen and attendants' compartments, and two first-class private dining compartments. The cooking is carried out by means of a gas range.

The first-class carriages are finished in figured Spanish mahogany, relieved with gold, the interiors being trimmed with morocco, moquette, terra cotta, tashmere velvet, and green cloth, finished in mahogany, and decorated with photographs of places of interest and the company's system. A similar design is adopted in the case of the third-class carriages, except that they are finished in polished teakwood, with lincrusta panels and dado. All the floors throughout the train are covered with figured cork matting, and a rug is supplied to each first-class compartment.

The buffet cars which it is intended to run are a distinct novelty. They contain a superb buffet, panelled and moulded in figured Spanish mahogany, and relieved with proof etchings and bevelled mirrors. The roof is treated with lincrusta, with a border picked out in gold.

The company have adopted new colours for the exteriors of all the coaches. The upper panels are now of French gray, and the lower brown, varnished and picked out in gold lines, and lettered and emblazoned with the company's new coat of arms. The carriages were designed by Mr. T. Parker, jun., the company's carriage and waggon superintendent, under whose direction they have been built.

As early as seven o'clock, yesterday morning a small army of officials and servants gathered on the main platform at Manchester, but it was not until 20 minutes before the time of its departure that the "special" was backed into the station. By this time one or two of the intending passengers had arrived, and the first to board the train was Sir Leader Williams, one of the engineers for the Manchester Ship Canal, who was accompanied by Lady Williams.

A great many of the guests had, however, travelled to London on the previous day, and the number of passengers was not quite so large as had been anticipated, scarcely 40 persons entering the luxuriously furnished coaches. Flowering plants in great profusion were placed upon the tiny tables, and the interior of the train afforded a striking contrast to the driving storm of rain and snow in which Manchester was at this time enveloped.

Mr. Richard Barker, the outdoor superintendent, who undertook the charge of the train on its first journey, escorted the guests to their places, and to the score or so of the general public who had assembled on the platform the object of greatest interest was the powerful engine, which had been gaily decorated with flags, and proudly bore in front the company's new coat of arms and the Royal arms. Punctually at eight o'clock the train steamed out of the station amid a perfect fusillade from a score of detonators which had been placed on the line.

For the first half hour or so the journey was dismal in the extreme, but, Woodhead tunnel safely passed, the sun shone at its brightest, and the external conditions became more in harmony with those which prevailed in the interior of the carriages.

The special train from Sheffield left under similar circumstances shortly after ten, and among the 70 passengers were the Lord Mayor of the city (Ald. W. E. Clegg).

DEPARTURE FROM NOTTINGHAM

The special constituting the first train out of Nottingham was timed to leave Arkwright-street Station at five minutes past ten o'clock this morning. This point of departure had, of course, to be utilised owing to the fact that the Central Station is not yet sufficiently advanced towards completion to admit of its being used.

Prior to the starting of the Nottingham special the two earlier trains, from Manchester and Sheffield respectively, had to pass through, and in this connection an unforeseen hitch occurred in relation to the arrangements. The Manchester train had to be pulled up for some three-quarters of an hour owing to slight over-heating of an axle. This, of course, necessitated a corresponding delay at Sheffield and Nottingham. The first train passed through Arkwright-street Station at 10.25, and the second at 10.34, both engines being decorated with flags.

Outside the station little or no excitement prevailed, although passers-by regarded with interest the spacious booking hall, the entrance to which was jealously guarded by the railway police and porters, no one being allowed even upon the platform without a permit.

It was nearly 20 minutes to eleven before the train destined to convey the Nottingham visitors to the Metropolis appeared round the sharp curve from the Central Station, and steamed up to the platform. Like those which had preceded it, the fore part of the engine was decorated with flags, six Union Jacks being fixed to the front and to the funnel. In addition were prominently displayed the coat of arms of the Great Central Company, emblazoned upon a green shield, and in front of all were the Royal Arms. The engine, an eight-wheeled bogie of the latest pattern, was attached to the train comprising four first-class carriages, a buffet car, and a third-class brake. The train was arranged throughout upon the corridor principle, the company's new and handsome coaches being requisitioned for the journey. Inside the appointments were upon the most complete scale.

As the train steamed out of the station the engine exploded twenty-four detonators which, placed upon the line at intervals of five yards apart, instituted a fitting salute of honour of the occasion.

The arrangements for the departure were in the hands of Mr. S. H. Fourdrinier, one of the superintendents of the company, who accompanied the train. He was assisted by the stationmaster, Mr. J. K. Shaw, who has been transferred from Penistone. Among those travelling by the train were the Sheriff of Nottingham (Councillor F. W. Gregory), Ald. Sir John Turney, Ald. J. Bright (deputy Mayor), Ald. Lambert, Ald. Sands, Ald. Bennett, Ald. J.P. Ford, Ald. Pullman, County Ald. R. Mellors, Ald. Renals, Ald. Blackburn, Mr. R. Fitzhugh, J.P. (chairman of the Watch Committee), Mr. J. T. McCraith, J.P., Mr. T. Potter, J.P., Mr. S. W. Johnson (loco. superintendent Midland Railway), Mr. E. Parry, M. I. C. E., Mr. Jesse Hind, J. P., Mr. Bornemann (Messrs. Ruston, Proctor and Co., Lincoln), Mr. T. D. Hancock, Mr. F. N. Ellis, Mr.

Arnold Lupton (Shirebrook), Mr. T. Mein (South Normanton), Mr. J. A. Longden (Manager of Stanton Ironworks), Mr. R. H. Beaumont (secretary Nottingham Chamber of Commerce).

It was about 22 minutes to eleven that the train left Nottingham to the accompaniment of a fusillade of fog signals, Loughborough was reached four minutes before the hour. Here the Mayor (Ald. Huram Coltman), the Town Clerk (Mr. John Jarrett), the Borough Surveyor (Mr. A. H. Walker), and Mr. W. Edward Woolley, all of whom had received invitations to attend the opening ceremony, joined the company.

No one was allowed on the platform without special permission, and amongst those who enjoyed that privilege were the Deputy Town Clerk (Mr. J. Ernest Jarrett), Mr. W. A. Cartwright, J.P., Mr. J. A. Sanders, Mr. J. H. Tyler, Mr. L. Watkin, Mr. George Hodson, Mr. G. Clements, Mr. John Paget, and a number of ladies. The stationmaster (Mr. T. W. Lee) was in attendance, with his staff, and the police arrangements were in the hands of Deputy Chief Constable Smith of the county constabulary, and Detective-Inspector Whitehouse for the railway company's police, from Sheffield.

At twelve minutes past eleven the train ran into Leicester, where, among others, the Mayor (Ald. Clifton, J.P.), the Town Clerk (Mr. Jos. Bell), and Ald. Lennard, J.P., were received.

A twenty minutes stoppage occurred outside Rugby owing to the axles of the dining saloon on the Sheffield train having become heated, a contingency which the officials had endeavoured to guard against by keeping the rolling stock in constant use for a period of three or four months past.

At Woodford and Brackley, at both of which places the occasion seemed to be commemorated by public holiday, the station premises were gaily decorated, and at the latter the local band and the fire brigade were on parade on the platform.

The Metropolitan system was joined just upon one o'clock, and Marylebone, bright with bunting, was reached about a quarter past two, after a most successful journey, the coaches running with the minimum of oscillation and vibration, while the weather all the way up was delightful.

THE LUNCHEON

Following upon the arrival of the guests, luncheon was served in an improvised banqueting hall on the station premises, to which close upon 800 invitations had been issued. In the absence of Earl Wharncliffe, Mr. Chapman, deputy-chairman of the company presided, and the chief officials of the Great Central and other companies present were - Mr. William Pollitt (general manager), Mr. O. S. Holt (secretary), Mr. R. B. M. Lingard-Monk (solicitor), Mr. F. Williams (accountant), Mr. C. R. Rowlandson (engineer), Mr. Harry Pollitt (locomotive engineer), Mr. R. Haig Brown (superintendent of the line), Mr. C. T. Smith (goods manager), Mr. E. Watkin (mineral manager), Mr. T. Parker, jun. (carriage and waggon superintendent), Mr. J. Rostern (assistant general manager), Mr. H. A. Ivatt (locomotive engineer, Great Northern Railway), Mr. A. Ross (engineer, Great Northern Railway), Mr. S. W. Johnson (locomotive superintendent, Midland Railway), Mr. J. A. Macdonald (engineer, Midland Railway).

The following were among the principal guests invited from Nottinghamshire, Derbyshire, Lincolnshire, and Leicestershire: - Lord Burton, Lord Heneage, the Hon. E. Chandos Leigh, Q.C., Sir G. Ernest Paget, Bart. (chairman of the Midland Railway Company), Mr. G. H. Turner (general manager), Sir John Turney (Nottingham), Sir Thomas and Lady Wright (Leicester), Sir Israel Hart (Leicester), Sir J. F. L. and Lady Rolleston (Leicester), Colonel Hutton, C.B. (director of the Great Central Railway), Mr. T. Bayley, M.P., Ald. G. Doughty, M.P., Mr. Walter Hazell, M.P., Mr. J. A. Jacoby, M.P., Mr. J. E. Johnson-Ferguson, M.P., Mr. J. W. Logan, M.P., Mr. C.B. McLaren, M.P., Colonel Sidebottom, M.P., Mr. J. H. Yoxall, M.P., Mr. B. Douglas, J.P. (Mayor of Chesterfield), Mr. Charles Markham and Mr. John Middleton (Chesterfield), Mr. W. Southworth (Mayor of Grimsby), Mr. and Mrs. J. Sutcliffe (Grimsby), Mr. W. A. Gelder (Mayor of Hull), Mr. Henry Smith and Mr. Alderman W. A. Massy (Hull), Mr. James Bell (Town Clerk, Leicester), Mr. John Butcher, Mr. R. R. Blackwell, Ald. Lennard, Mr. E. G. Mawby, Mr. John Storey, Mr. J. S. Vorley, and Mr. J. Wilford (Leicester), Mr. Thomas Bell, J.P., and Mr. August Bornemann (Lincoln), Mr. T. I. Birkin, the Mayor of Nottingham (Ald. E. H. Fraser, D. C. L.), Mr. Fred. Acton, J.P., Mr. R. H. Beaumont (secretary Chamber of Commerce), Alderman C. Bennett, F. Pullman, J. Renals, A. Brownsword, G. Blackburn, J.P. Ford, and J. Bright. Mr. Brown (city engineer), Mr. F. Collins, Mr. Fitzhugh, J.P., Mr. Jesse Hind, Ald. Pullman, Mr. E. P. Hooley, Ald. Lambert, J.P., Mr. E. Lindley, Ald. Sands, J.P., Mr. Robert Mellors, Mr. C. Tylden-Wright, Mr. T. Potter, Mr. F. J. Turner, and Mr. Weinburg (Nottingham); Mr. A. Barnes (Chesterfield), Mr. H. Blundell (Ilkeston), Mr. T. H. Boam (Derby), Mr. H. Bollard (Leicester), Mr. P. M. Chesters (Ilkeston), Mr. M. Deacon (Sheepbridge), Mr. R. Eddison (Shireoaks), Mr. F. N. Ellis, J.P. (Nottingham), Mr. H. Fisher (Clifton Colliery, Nottingham), Mr. T. H. Gray (Linby), Mr. T. D. Hancock (Nottingham), Mr. J.P. Houfton (Bolsover), Mr. J. H. Humble (Staveley), Mr. W. H. Lancaster

(Bestwood), Mr. J. A. Longden (Stanton), Mr. M. Lyon (Annesley), Mr. John Lancaster (Bestwood), Mr. Walter Salmond (Alfreton), Mr. J. S. Sampson (Pilsley), Mr. G. L. Marshall (Shipley), Mr. F. Huntsman and Mr. G. Marshall (Retford), and Mr. W. T. Rowlatt (Leicester).

The Earl of Wharncliffe, who was present during the early portion of the proceedings, apologised from the chair for his inability to preside on account of illness, and, in the course of a few remarks, alluded to the successful inauguration of the undertaking. It was, he supposed, the last important line to be run into London, and he could only hope that, like all "lasts", it would be the best. (Cheers.)

Upon the conclusion of the sumptuous banquet the Deputy-Chairman briefly submitted the loyal toasts, which were duly honoured, and afterwards proposed the health of the Right Hon. C. T. Ritchie, M.P. It was, he said, felt by himself and his colleagues that when they were adding a new trunk line to the already existing lines to London it would only be fitting and appropriate if it could be opened and inaugurated by the Minister who represented the great trading interests of the country. (Hear, Hear.) They therefore approached Mr. Ritchie, and he at once kindly undertook to perform the ceremony which he would shortly be asked to do.

He did not propose to enter into a description of the line, but he wished to draw especial attention to one or two facts which were unique in themselves. The new line was the greatest railway, constituted and opened as one undertaking, that had been authorised by Parliament for more than 50 years. (Applause.) They had spent twelve millions of money on the undertaking, and of these twelve millions four had been spent in London. Then, during the course of the evidence which came before Parliamentary Committee of both Houses in 1891 and 1892, it became abundantly clear that what would probably be the last railway entering London from the North, for the vast space that was required for a terminus, with its necessary accommodation for all classes of traffic, passengers, merchandise, and coal, was not to be found between Paddington on the west and Liverpool-street on the east.

As concerned the undertaking itself, the enormous growth of trade in the country which made such demands upon the resources of railways amply justified the venture, and that point he wished to emphasise. Since it was sanctioned by Parliament in 1892 the increase of railway traffic receipts in Great Britain, down to 1897, had been no less than the gigantic sum of £11,284,444, while the five great trunk lines running into London, the Great Eastern, the Great Northern, the Midland, the London and North-Western, and the Great Western, had increased to no less an extent than £5,219,834. He only mentioned those figures to show that there was room for the Great Central. The system had been compared to the letter "T", but he would rather liken it to a tree, with its roots firmly planted in London, and its trunk gracefully growing through the Midland Counties to Sheffield, and from there its branches spreading to Grimsby on the east coast and Liverpool on the west, with one or two feelers in Yorkshire and Lincolnshire. (Applause.)

He could not bring his remarks to a close without drawing attention to the fact that the credit of the inception of the scheme was due to the indomitable energy and genius of one man, and that man was Sir Edward Watkin - (Cheers) - and he congratulated him that he had lived to see the completion of the undertaking of which he was the father. (Renewed cheers.)

There was another man who he must not omit, and upon whom had devolved the burden of carrying out the undertaking in all its multifarious details - the most excellent general manager, Mr. William Pollitt. (Cheers.) He was a man of the highest ability, and he could only say that his talents had been laid at the service of the Great Central Railway Company with a self-sacrificing devotion to its interests which only those who knew him could thoroughly appreciate or understand. He believed that the undertaking had added many lines to that gentleman's forehead, but he trusted that the success which would attend it would add many years to his life. (Cheers.) He thought Mr. Pollitt's motto had been "Pluck, Prudence, Perseverance," and no man deserved more richly than he did the sight of a prosperous issue to the scheme for whose fulfilment he had worked with such indomitable energy. (Hear, hear.)

It would be invidious to mention other names, but he must say that the engineers and contractors had done well, as it was evidenced by the fact that, notwithstanding the terrible disorganisation and trouble caused by the engineers' strike and other labour difficulties, they had completed their work in the astonishingly short time of less than four years, a fact which reflected infinite credit upon all concerned.

In conclusion, it was his pleasing duty to present to Mr. Ritchie, on behalf of the directors of the Great Central, a plan of the railway engrossed on vellum, illuminated with the arms of the company, and with those of the right hon. gentleman, and he hoped Mr. Ritchie would accept it and treasure it as a little momento of the occasion, and a slight token of goodwill of the Board of Directors. The plan would be enclosed in a silver casket, also inscribed with the same arms and monograms. He begged Mr. Ritchie's acceptance of the gift, and asked the company to drink heartily to his health.

The toast having been warmly received, Mr. Ritchie, who was loudly cheered on rising, said that he assured the company that the scene which had just been presented to him was, on his part, a most unexpected one, and a most welcome one - (Hear, hear) - and he returned to the deputy-chairman and his colleagues his grateful thanks for not only the kind expressions which had been used with regard to himself, but also for the extremely substantial and pleasing manner in which they had given visiole expression to their feelings. The splendid token of the event which they had presented to him and his, and they would always regard it as a very pleasing memorial of a most agreeable occasion. (Hear, hear.)

He knew that he was indebted for the honour which they had done him in asking him to perform the ceremony, not because of any personal qualification of his own, but because he was at the head of the great Department which had such close relations with railway companies, (Hear, hear.) Those relations were close and, he was glad to think, friendly. (Applause.) It was true that they at the Board of Trade sometimes had to make representations to railway companies, with regard to which they did not always see eye to eye. (Loud laughter.) But still the railway companies recognised that the Board of Trade had a great public duty to perform, and so long as they believed that they were attempting to serve no particular interest, but only the great public interest, he was glad to think that those representations were received in a friendly manner, however disagreeable some of them might be. (Laughter and cheers.)

But the disagreeable points were largely overcome by the many agreeable communications which they had with each other, and the directors of the Great Central had conferred a great honour upon him in asking him to perform the most agreeable duty of starting the first train from that great metropolitan centre away to the north. (Applause.) They had charged him not only with the duty of returning his own personal thanks to the directors, but also with the pleasant duty of asking the company to drink a toast, a bumper toast it must be - "Success to the Great Central Railway." (Cheers.)

The deputy-chairman had already remarked upon what he thought they were entitled to consider a great fact, namely, that there was little probability of such a scene as that ever occurring again; there was but little probability that any great trunk railway would ever again seek entrance into the Metropolis. There seemed to be little room for any such enterprise, for the physical difficulties of securing a site in the Metropolis for any great trunk line now were such as to render it most improbable, if not altogether impossible, that they would ever again see a scene like that commemorating the entrance of a great railway into London.

There were one or two reflections which he thought on an occasion of that kind were not out of place, and which he would venture to give expression to. It would be perhaps a matter of surprise and astonishment to many present to hear that of all the existing great network of railways in the Metropolis not one were in being when her Majesty came to the throne. London was at that time a great metropolis, and yet there was no railway station in it, with one exception, and that exception was so trifling that it was hardly worthy of note, inasmuch as it was a small railway from Minories to Blackwall, drawn by a rope. (Laughter.)

It was not until the year1838 that any attempt was made by a great railway company to seek admission to the Metropolis, and the first to make that attempt was what was known as the Great Western, which in the year he had named made a railway between Paddington and Maidenhead. So much astonishment and curiosity did that novel enterprise create amongst those through whose district the line ran that he was told a great posse of police had to be stationed along the route to prevent the Eton boys from invading it. (Laughter.)

The next line, which, he thought, was made in the following September, was the London and North-Western's - then the London to Birmingham -

incursion into Euston, but even then the line was only worked by locomotives as far as Camden Town, thence to Euston Square the trains were drawn by a rope.

The next railway which sought entrance to London was the London and Colchester line in the year 1843. Afterwards it became the Eastern Counties, and then the Great Eastern.

Then for seven years no further steps were taken by any company until the Great Northern opened their line 1850, and 18 more years elapsed - he was, of course, speaking of railways from the North - ere the Midland began to run into London. At that time, 30 years ago, the Midland was the baby railway from the North. (Laughter.) He was told that there was no christening such as that at its birth, but that it contented itself by stating that the first train started from London at 6.15 a.m. - that was all the ceremony performed. (Laughter.)

But they were glad to think, because it had some bearing upon the fortunes of the Great Central, that the child of those early days had developed into such vigorous manhood as the Midland had done to-day - (Cheers) - and he thought they were justified in considering that the success which had attended it was a good augury, a happy augury, to the success of the Great Central. (Cheers.)

Before the Midland obtained access to the Metropolis it carried thirteen millions and a quarter passengers, and its gross earnings came to something like £3,000,000. In 1897 it carried 47 and a half million passengers, while its gross earnings were £10,000,000. (Applause.) He thought that the Midland people were right in considering that that enormous increase in their earning power and in their traffic was due to the extension to London. It was difficult to say precisely how much of their increased prosperity was due to that fact, but if they compared it to an existing line which had entrance to London, and contrasted its development with that of the Midland, he thought there was some justification for believing that it was to the entrance into the Metropolis of the Midland that the large development of its traffic was mainly attributable. He found that during the same number of years, the London and North-Western's increase amounted to 88 per cent., and the Midland's to 220 per cent., and therefore he thought they were justified in considering that its extension to London gave a great stimulus to the traffic throughout the whole Midland system. (Applause.)

He had no doubt that the question which had often been anxiously asked by those responsible for the making and administration of that line had been, was there room for another line into London? Well, when they came to consider the enormous progress which had been made in population and in trade during the period of 30 years, in which there had been no entrance sought to the Metropolis by any railway company from the north, he thought that they must also come to the conclusion that those who were responsible for that line were justified in believing that the time had arrived when they might with confidence seek that entrance into London, without which it was impossible for their system adequately to be developed. (Applause.)

London had increased in that period of 30 years from three and a half millions to over six millions of inhabitants, and the increase which had taken place there had had a corresponding increase in all the great trading and industrial centres which were served by the Great Central line. So that, taking the question of increase of population and also the great increase in the trade and commerce of the country, he thought they were justified in assuming that there was a great future before their line. (Cheers.)

Again, if they looked at another point of the question and saw the enormous congestion which undoubtedly existed in all the railways coming to London from the North, in addition to the enormous cost which must be entailed upon existing companies by extending their lines, he thought they would agree with him that the Great Central were justified in the course which they had taken. (Hear, hear.)

The Great Central, as he had said, had access to a large number of the great industrial centres, but hitherto their traffic had been not from north to south, but from east to west, and when they desired to send their traffic south, they had to send it, after travelling, perhaps, but a few miles over their own system, to some other railway to be conveyed to the Metropolis. That state of things was not an agreeable one for the M. S. and L., and it was, therefore, no wonder that they should desire that the profits arising from this traffic should go into their own coffers rather than into the coffers of their neighbours. They had been crippled for the want of a London terminus, but they had now got that terminus, and all the difficulty would cease.

They had communication with the docks in Liverpool, and with their own docks at Grimsby, and he could not doubt that the facilities which were afforded them by means of communication with London and with all the great towns which they tapped in their system was a happy augury for the success of the undertaking in which they were engaged.

It was a line also which had gone through much tribulation. He imagined that there was no railway of modern times that had had to overcome so much Parliamentary difficulty as the Great Central. (Hear, hear.) But it had overcome these difficulties by much perseverance, and he was glad that the deputy-chairman had pointed out that the main credit for the success of the scheme was due to Sir Edward Watkin - (Cheers) - whom they were all proud and delighted to see there that day to witness the crowning of the work which had occupied so much of a busy life. (Cheers.)

He was glad, too, that Mr. Chapman had not omitted the name of a gentleman who, perhaps, next to Sir Edward Watkin, deserved the most credit for the manner in which the great enterprise had been carried out - he meant the General Manager, Mr. Pollitt. (Cheers.) He was told that not only did Mr. Pollitt deserve the highest praise for the carrying out of the plans which had been settled upon for the line, but that he was the man upon whom devolved the lion's share of the work in overcoming the Parliamentary difficulties. (Applause.) No one could look at the changes which had taken place in that particular district without feeling that enormous credit must be due to the general manager. He had waved his magic wand, and all those enticing villas and pleasant shades - (Laughter) - which used at one time to exist in that neighbourhood had disappeared, to give place to a network of railways. The energy which has been imported into the inception and the creation of that line deserved success, and he believed that he was not too optimistic when he said that it would secure it. (Hear, hear.)

He thought that, without wishing any harm to any other line of railway, he might be permitted to hope that the Great Central would experience the utmost success which those who were immediately connected with it could possibly desire, and he was satisfied that if it did not meet with that success, it would fill a great public want and would make a return which would be satisfactory alike to the proprietors and the public. He begged, therefore, to propose success to the undertaking. (Cheers.)

Mr. Littler, C.B., Q.C., proposed the health of the deputy-chairman, and in doing so sketched the history of the company during the past quarter of a century a history, which, he said, had been one series of struggles, culminating in a Parliamentary fight which he did not hesitate to describe as the greatest which had taken place on the part of any railway company since 1845.

Mr. Chapman having briefly acknowledged the compliment, the proceedings ended.

THE OPENING CEREMONY

Shortly afterwards Mr. Ritchie performed the ceremony of starting the first corridor train, consisting of six coaches, with guards van, officially sanctioned by the Board of Trade. The right hon. gentleman signalled the departure, and applied the lever which gave impetus to the train, which, driven by Mr. Harry Pollitt, locomotive engineer, moved out of the station to the cheers of the assembled company. Later the guests were privileged to inspect the proportions and appointments of the Hotel Great Central, the base of which was occupied by the Band of the Coldstream Guards, who also supplied music during the luncheon.

The return Nottingham train left at 5.45, and running to schedule time throughout arrived at ten minutes after nine.

THE ENGINEERS AND CONTRACTORS

For the purpose of facilitating the construction of the tenth and last great trunk line to the Metropolis, the Great Central Company divided their extension into three divisions, the northern with nearly 52 miles, the southern with 42, and the metropolitan with two. It is a matter of common knowledge that over the northern division Mr. Edward Parry, M. Inst. C. E., of Nottingham, had the sole direction, while Sir Douglas Fox, V.P. Inst. C. E., and Mr. Francis Fox, M. Inst. C. E., were the engineers-in-chief for the southern and metropolitan sections. Sir Douglas Fox also holds the position of consulting engineer to the company, and Mr. Alexander Ross, KM. Inst. C. E., and Mr. C. A. Rowlandson, M. Inst. C. E., the former and present chief engineers for the company, exercised occasional supervision over the whole route.

The first contract, covering nearly 20 miles, from Annesley to East Leake, was let to Messrs. Logan and Hemingway, and the second, which commenced in the parish of Normanton-on-Soar, and extended a distance of 16½ miles to the south side of Leicester, to Mr. Henry Lovatt, of Wolverhampton, who is now concerned with the erection of the Nottingham Central Station for the Great Central and Great Northern Railway Joint Companies, under a sub-contract from Messrs. Logan and Hemingway. For rather less than 16 miles, the intermediate distance between Aylestone and Rugby, the responsible contractors were Messrs. Topham, Jones, and Railton, of Westminster.

At Rugby the northern division ended, and it may be added that amongst a loyal and courteous staff Mr. Parry had the assistance of Mr. H. E. Allen and Mr. A. A. Barker on the first section, while Mr. C. R. Hemingway was the resident partner of the contracting firm. The resident engineers on the second section were Messrs. Sharp and Ashworth at Loughborough, and Mr. Chalcraft at Leicester, while Mr. J. A. Mousley acted as Mr. Lovatt's principal agent.

Messrs. Thomas Oliver and Sons, of Rugby, secured contract No.4, from Rugby to the south of Woodford and Hinton Station, a distance of rather more than sixteen miles, and in addition to the construction of the main line, were called upon to lay down a branch railway, of 35 chains, south of Woodford connecting with the East and West Junction Railway, from Towcester to Stratford-on-Avon, at Byfield. Mr. A. W. H. Casson was the resident engineer, and Mr. W. Watson and Mr. W. R. Morris were the engineers for the contractors.

Twenty-four and a half miles of main line, a three-quarters of a mile loop to the East and West Junction, and a branch, 8¼ miles in length, from Eydon Junction to the Great Western Company's main line at Banbury, were comprised within contracts five and six, let to Messrs. Walter Scott and Co., of Newcastle and Westminster. Mr. J. T. Middleton was the resident partner at Brackley, and supervised the whole of the work, being aided by Mr. T. Thomson, Mr. T. T. Middleton, Mr. W. T. Pickering, Mr. Colin Smith, and Mr. P. Riach.

Messrs. Walter Scott and Co. carried the extension to its connection with the Metropolitan at Quainton-road, and the remaining contract, covering the two miles from Finchley-road to the Marylebone terminus, was entrusted to Mr. J. T. Firbank, M.P., of London. Mr. Edmund Wragge, M. Inst. C. E., was the resident engineer for the metropolitan division, and he had the advantage of the co-operation of Mr. G. A. Hobson, M. Inst. C. E., chief assistant to Sir Douglas and Mr. Francis Fox who prepared the drawings and designs for the bridges, &c., on the stretch from Rugby and of Mr. H. W. Braddock, the firm's architectural assistant who designed the terminus buildings, and the country stations.

Engineers and contractors alike have, with uniform courtesy, afforded every facility for viewing the works and obtaining the information needed to complete the description of a notable undertaking.

THE RIGHT HON. THE EARL OF WHARNCLIFFE

The Earl of Wharncliffe, who succeeded to the position of chairman of directors upon the retirement of Sir Edward Watkin, has been for a long period connected with the company, for he became a director so long ago as 1864.

He was born in 1827, succeeded to the title of Baron Wharncliffe in 1876, being at the same time created Viscount Carlton and Earl of Wharncliffe. He was formerly a lieutenant in the Grenadier Guards, holds the office of honorary colonel of the 1st. Volunteer Battalion York and Lancaster Regiment, and is a D. L. and J. P. for the West Riding of York, and a J. P. for county Forfar.

When the first sod of the extension was cut at Alpha-road, in November 1894 his lordship made the frank admission that when the idea of the new line was first mooted he was not struck with the notion, and did not expect to see the realisation of the project. Happily his lordship's doubts have been dispelled, and, still in his position at the head of the company, he has witnessed the full fruition of an undertaking which in the early stages was beset with many seemingly insuperable difficulties.

MR. WILLIAM POLLITT

Next to Sir Edward Watkin, the former chairman of the company, no one has played a more prominent part in the promotion of the extension of the Great Central system than Mr. William Pollitt, the general manager.

Upon the several occasions of Parliamentary inquiries his was the corporate evidence in relation to main details, and it may be said that to a large extent he carried the case for the company by his own evidence. Mr. Pollitt's examination and cross-examination at the many sittings of the Committee were of a most exhaustive character. Speaking from long experience, he was forcible in his advocacy of the claims of the company to Parliamentary sanction, which was ultimately obtained.

Mr. Pollitt has more than once been, deservedly, the recipient of well-earned compliments at the hands of the directors, who have in substantial ways shown their sense of the value of his services.

SIR DOUGLAS FOX, V.P., INST. C. E.

Sir Douglas Fox, V.P., Inst. C. E., and Mr. Francis Fox, M. Inst. C. E., the engineers of the Southern and Metropolitan divisions of the new line, are the sons of, and were partners of, the late Sir Charles Fox.

Sir Douglas Fox is now the senior vice-president of the Institution of Civil Engineers, and will in due course be the president of the institution.

For nearly 40 years they have been busily engaged upon railway works in many parts of the world. They were engineers of the Cape Town and Wellington Railway, and more recently - jointly with Sir Charles Metcalfe - of the Rhodesia Railways, and of the South Indian Railway jointly with Sir George Bruce.

They were also engineers of the High Level Joint Railways in South London, of the Mersey Railway (jointly with the late Sir James Brunlees), the Liverpool Overhead Railway (jointly with the late Mr. Greathead), as well as the Manchester Central, the Chester and Connahs Quay and Hawarden Bridge.

They also act for the Cardiff Railways, and have carried out many foreign and colonial railways in Queensland, Argentine Republic, and Brazil.

Mr. Francis Fox was also one of the three technical commissioners for the Simplon Tunnel.

MR. EDWARD PARRY, M. INST. C. E.

Mr. Edward Parry, M. Inst. C. E., the chief engineer of that part of the line which stretches from Annesley to Rugby, was articled, in early youth, to a firm who were the engineers for several railways in North Wales, and during his novitiate he was engaged upon a portion of the Wrexham, Mold, and Connah's Quay Railway, and also upon the Mold and Denbigh Railway, which is now worked by the London and North-Western Company.

Upon the completion of the Mold and Denbigh line, Mr. Parry joined the staff of the Midland Railway Company, under the late Mr. Crossley, who was engineer-in-chief to the company. After being at Derby some time he was transferred to Nuneaton to take part in the work connected with a line which the Midland Company were making between Ashby and Nuneaton, in conjunction with the London and North-Western Company. He remained there for several months, and was then sent to the Settle and Carlisle Railway, which was just then being commenced, and which, being on the main line to Scotland, was an undertaking of considerable importance. Mr. Parry was assistant engineer there for two or three years, afterwards returning to Derby, and remaining at the head office for some time.

In 1874 Mr. Parry was appointed resident engineer of the northern part of the Nottingham and Melton line, which was then being commenced. The line was completed in 1877 and shortly afterwards Mr. Parry was appointed county surveyor of Nottinghamshire. This appointment enabled him to commence private practice as a civil engineer, and since his retirement, upon the formation of the County Council, from the official position he has been engaged in much important railway work.

He suggested the course of the Dore and Chinley Railway, which was taken over by the Midland, he and Mr. Story, of Derby, being joint engineers of the line.

About this period Mr. Parry was commissioned to prepare plans for the Nottingham Suburban Railway, which he carried out with marked success, and in 1883 he was first asked to take some preliminary levels for the extension of the M. S. L. Co.'s line to London.

It was not, however, until 1887 that Mr. Liddell, who was acting as chief engineer for the extension, was instructed to lay out the northern part of the line from Beighton to Annesley. Mr. Parry, acted with Mr. Liddell in preparing the whole of the plans for that portion of the line, and subsequently in preparing the whole of the plans of the line from Annesley to London.

Upon the M. S. and L. Company's Bill receiving Parliamentary assent, Mr. Parry was appointed chief engineer of that portion of the line from Annesley to Rugby, the other section, from Rugby to Quainton-road, as well as the metropolitan portion of the line, being under the supervision of Sir Douglas Fox and Mr. Francis Fox.

MR. J. W. LOGAN, M.P.,

MR. C. R. HEMINGWAY,

MR. FREDERICK COLLINS.

MR. J. W. LOGAN, M.P.

Messrs. Logan and Hemingway, who were responsible for the first section on the extension, that from Annesley to East Leake, possess a long and honourable record in regard to railway construction, and works of a like character. For upwards of half-a-century the firm and its immediate predecessors have been concerned in vast undertakings in all parts of the kingdom.

The business had its inception so far back as the early '40's, during the erection of the famous Congleton viaduct, on the North Stafford Railway. In that instance Messrs. Hemingway and Pearson and Rennie and Logan were engaged on the masonry work, and in 1846 Messrs. Hemingway and Pearson were contractors for masonry at the Britannia Tubular bridge crossing Menai Straits.

Shortly after the firms were merged into one, and when in 1865 the late Mr. James Hemingway became a partner with Mr. John Logan, sen., the style of Logan and Hemingway was adopted.

Meanwhile they had been concerned with extensive dock works at Newport, and the construction of the Newport tunnel on the Great Western Railway, as well as the laying down of a portion of the same company's South Wales line to Bridgend.

Among other contracts were the erection of the temporary bridge over the Thames at Blackfriars, whilst the new structure was being built, work on the Shipley and Guiseley, Otley and Ilkley, Knutsford and Altrincham, and Buxton to Rowsley, Taunton and Chard, Stockport and Timperley sections, at East Bute Dock, Cardiff, Penarth Dock, Caerphilly Tunnel, and on the Abergavenny to Hereford Railway.

From 1869 until 1878 the firm did a large amount of work for what was then the Manchester, Sheffield and Lincolnshire Railway Company, in the neighbourhood of Sheffield and Rotherham, including the Tinsley and Rotherham extension, additions to the Victoria Station, Sheffield, the Chapeltown branch, and the Darnall curve. At the same time they were called upon to execute a contract in respect of the Alexandra Dock at Grimsby, which was opened by the Prince of Wales in 1879, in addition to the construction of a joint line for the North Stafford and the Manchester, Sheffield and Lincolnshire from Macclesfield to Marple.

During the same years Messrs. Logan and Hemingway were employing a large

MR. C. R. HEMINGWAY   MR. FREDERICK COLLINS

*number of men on the Tilton and Market Harborough line, and on the northern part
of the L. and N. W. line from Saxondale to Stathern, through Bingham-road, as well
as another branch for the M. S., and L. at Widness.*

*In the early eighties the St. Pancras connecting line with the new goods station,
and a dry dock at Cardiff claimed their attention, which in 1884 was transferred to
the laying down of a mineral line, on the Holwell branch and extension near Melton
Mowbray.*

*During the latter part of 1887 Messrs. Logan and Hemingway started various
contracts in Cardiff and the neighbourhood, including the Penarth and Barry Junction
Railway and the bridge over the River Taff at Grangetown, which was opened by the
Duke of Clarence and named after him.*

*In 1888 they widened the Midland line between Elstree tunnel and the Welsh
Harp, Hendon, and made the Chester to Connahs Quay Railway.*

*Early in 1890 the firm commenced operations on the northern part of the M. S.,
and L. Company's extension from Beighton to Heath, via Chesterfield and Staveley,
a contract which, together with colliery branches, involved the construction of nearly
30 miles of railway. At the conclusion of this undertaking Messrs. Logan and
Hemingway secured the contract for the section which they have just completed.*

*Of the present members of the firm Mr. J. W. Logan, M.P., joined about 1867, and
became a partner in about 1873, while Mr. C. R. Hemingway was taken into
partnership in 1882, three years after the death of his father.*

*Mr. Frederick Collins, whose portrait we also publish, has been connected with the
firm for nearly 50 years. His name is universally known in contracting circles. Upon
Mr. Collins, as manager for Messrs. Logan and Hemingway, duties of the most
important and arduous character have devolved during the period of the carrying out
of the contract, and has been brought to so successful an issue.*

MR. WALTER SCOTT

Mr. Walter Scott is head of the firm of Messrs. Walter Scott and Co., of Newcastle and Westminster, who were entrusted with contracts No. 5 and 6, covering 24½ miles of main line, a loop line three-quarters of a mile at Woodford, forming the south junction with the East and West Junction Railway, and a branch of 8¼ miles from near Eydon to the Great Western main line to the north of Banbury Station, making altogether 33½ miles.

MR. HENRY LOVATT

Mr. Henry Lovatt, of Wolverhampton, whose portrait we publish, was entrusted with Contract No. 2, which included the Loughborough and Leicester sections, a length which necessitated much responsible work.

APPENDIX

Conversion Tables

Length

12 inches	= 1 foot	= 0.305 metres
3 feet	= 1 yard	= 0.91 metres
22 yards	= 1 chain	= 20.12 metres
10 chains	= 1 furlong	= 0.20 kilometres
8 furlongs	= 1 mile (1,760 yds.)	= 1.61 kilometres

Square Measurement

144 square inches	= 1 square foot	= 0.092 square metres
9 square feet	= 1 square yard	= 0.836 square metres
1,210 square yards	= 1 rood	= 1,011.71 sq. metres
4 roods	= 1 acre (4,840 sq.yds.)	= 4,046.86 sq.m. (0.405 hectares)
640 acres	= 1 square mile	= 2.59 sq. kilometres (259 hectares)

Cubic Measurement

1,728 cubic inches	= 1 cubic foot	= 0.028 cubic metres
27 cubic feet	= 1 cubic yard	= 0.764 cubic metres

Avoirdupois Weight

16 ounces	= 1 pound	= 0.454 kilograms
14 pounds	= 1 stone	= 6.35 kilograms
2 stones	= 1 quarter	= 12.70 kilograms
4 quarters	= 1 hundredweight	= 50.80 kilograms
20 hundredweights	= 1 ton (2,240 lbs.)	= 1,016 kgs. (1.016 tonnes)

Liquid Measurement

4 gills	= 1 pint	= 0.568 litres
2 pints	= 1 quart	= 1.137 litres
4 quarts	= 1 gallon	= 4.546 litres